# MY LIFE WITH THE BIG BOYS

## Kim De Paola

Published by Mediacasters Publishing House

ISBN: 979-8-9885175-4-2

# DEDICATION

This is dedicated to my "BIG BOYS",
the ones that shaped me and led me to
the place I was meant to be.

Dorothy

Elvira

Gussy

Butchie

Brian

Joey

Frank

George

Jimmy

Michael

And finally, To My Christopher

# TABLE OF CONTENTS

# FOREWORD

*by Dolores Catania*

In a world brimming with pretenders and wannabes, there stands a singular figure who defies imitation: Kim D. Her life is a tapestry of authentic experiences, woven with threads of resilience, courage, and uncompromising truth. While many boast of grand adventures and conquests they've never actually encountered, Kim D has not only lived these tales but has done so with a grace and strength that few can truly comprehend. She embodies the spirit of authenticity in an age where superficiality often reigns. Kim D is the real deal, the true big boy of life's grand stage, navigating its ups and downs with unwavering resolve and an unyielding sense of self.

This book is not just a testament to Kim D's remarkable journey but a celebration of a life lived fearlessly and truthfully. It's a tribute to her indomitable spirit, her capacity to turn challenges into triumphs, and her refusal to settle for anything less than her true self. Through her stories, may you find inspiration to pursue your own path with the same fervor and honesty. To Kim D, your story is an inspiration to us all, a shining example of what it means to live authentically and passionately. Here's to the real big boy deal, Kim D – may your journey continue to inspire and uplift all who have the privilege of knowing you.

*Dolores Catania*

 # FOREWORD

*by Jacqueline Laurita*

If you are a true fan of Bravo's "Real Housewives of New Jersey," then you must be familiar with the iconic, dramatic scenes from the Posche fashion shows, hosted by the one and only Kim D—everyone's favorite outspoken and notorious "villain."

When I first met Kim, I knew we would be friends. Not only was she fun to talk to and a joy to shop with at her store, but I also recognized right away that she was a straight shooter. I appreciate that quality in a friend. Sometimes the truth hurts, but at least with Kim, you know you're getting the truth. I recall only a couple of issues between us, and when I confronted her, she owned her part in it immediately, without apologies. Her ability to take accountability for her actions, and to do so in such a way that I couldn't even stay mad, was remarkable. She always had her reasons, whether I agreed with them or not, and she had a way of making them make sense.

But is she really a villain? Or is she a woman who has endured and survived a colorful, checkered past that most people can't even imagine? Where did she learn her intolerance for nonsense and her bravery to stand alone, sometimes against multiple adversaries, and speak her mind? Who are the "big boys" Kim has mentioned playing with? And how does she manage to look so damn good while doing it?

Can a dog lover with eight of her own and a loyal friend group that has lasted for decades really be all that bad?

As a friend of Kim's for over 16 years, I can tell you there's much more to Kim D than meets the eye. This book reveals many secrets, and in true Kim D fashion, she doesn't just share her own. Kim gets raw and opens up about her lifetime of grief, love, family, friendships, and her time in reality TV.

She's sharing her life lessons and speaking out in a way you've never heard before. Read her book — it will blow your mind.

Me and Teresa

# FOREWORD

*by Teresa Giudice*

Some people say that I am the REALEST reality television personality in the history of reality tv and I have to say that I agree with them. I am. Nobody has done what I have done, for as long as I have done it (14 years and counting) and have looked as good as I have looked while doing it. I'm kidding about that last part, but not really. The truth is I owe a lot of credit to Kim D. & her Posche store for my look during the old-school early days of 'Real Housewives of New Jersey'. When you think of that era, (you remember "prostitution whore" & the table flip), you have to acknowledge Kim D. & all of the shit that went down at those Posche Fashion Shows as being a MAJOR part of the success of RHONJ. The key to being a reality tv personality is … being REAL … and Kim D. is as real as it gets. Whether you love her (which I have in the past & currently do) or you hate her (which I have in the past & could again tomorrow), you can always count on Kim D. to tell you EXACTLY what is on her mind, whether you want to hear it or not. That's Kim D. (She also knows more gossip about 'The Real Housewives of New Jersey', so much more than the producers that I am surprised they haven't offered her a job yet) In closing, let me say one last thing about my friend Kim D. She is the: Powerful Original Shit-stirring Connected Housewife who is Elegant Love, Love, Love Teresa Giudice

#  FOREWORD

*by Siggy Flicker*

From the moment I met Kim D, I liked her. She was raw, honest, a hard worker and a straight shooter. I loved her mom too. She was a class act. I always felt that Kim D was used by production to "bring it" because so many cast members were so fake while filming. They needed Kim D to save seasons on RHONJ because they could edit her any way they wanted and she didn't care. She was a team player. When some would talk bad about Kim D, I always stuck up for her time and time again and that would irritate a few frauds because I couldn't be controlled. You see, for people like Kim D and I, we can't kiss ass. It's not in our DNA. We live our authentic selves and don't care to fit into any circle. I think it's because we were raised with moms who adored us and taught us to know our worth. Anyway, when it comes to Kim D, I feel she got the short end of the stick with RHONJ. They made so many useful idiots HW's who didn't and don't bring anything to show and never made a real legend to the RHONJ Francine a HW.

I love Kim D and will always stand by her.

*Siggy Flicker*

# 🫦 PROLOGUE

When I was on The Real Housewives of New Jersey, my life went viral. It was nothing I expected or understood at the time; however, I was ready to receive everything that the Housewives had to offer. After all, my experience here on Earth has been one adventure after another. Yet, this new adventure felt different. I knew something good was coming because the universe always has my back.

*"You are a midget, you are nothing. I play with the Big Boys."*

Silence.

And then the crowd went wild. My fame was catapulted into the stratosphere. This is because I speak the truth. I am real. If I did not own my truth and tell it like it is, I would be living half a life. Since the day I was born, I have danced on the razor's edge of drama, toxic relationships, and the illusion of love. While I navigated powerful lessons throughout my years, the most important lesson was that I had the ability to pursue whatever I wanted.

My mouth got me in trouble once in a while. Well, the truth is that my mouth ignites fireworks when I see injustices. One thing you need to know about me is that I do not tolerate people who manipulate and lie. If you want to be in my life, you have to be a person who stands behind their word. You need to stand for what you believe in. After all, if you stand for nothing, you fall for everything.

At times, I was my own worst enemy, and at other times, I was my very best friend. While I pride myself on telling the truth, I also know that the hardest part about truth-seeking is when you look in the mirror and see your own truth. My truth has not always been pretty, but it is mine to own. My lessons are yours to understand and unravel. We all have a common thread living here on Earth. There is pain, heartache, and then there is joy.

My life has been shaped by a series of "Big Boys" (including my mother), who encouraged my independence and ignited the confidence that you witnessed on RHONJ. I learned through hardship that I was enough. I understood that through the myriad of painful decisions, I grew closer to who I was born to be.

Confidence was not handed to me on a silver platter. I learned to be confident through trial and error. Helping me along the way were my "Big Boys." I was never told to be silent. I was never encouraged to be someone different than myself.

My "Big Boys" supported my voice and lit a fire in me. I was able to use my voice and claim my authenticity. Today, so many people are frightened of being themselves. We live in a trophy culture, where everyone is handed a gold medal for mediocre performance. In my opinion, the trophy culture should be abolished. We are teaching future generations that it is okay to be average. Listen to me: we all have the potential to be extraordinary.

This generation of entitled, loud-mouthed wannabes does not grasp the importance of living through difficult times. Without darkness in life, we cannot see the light. Without understanding the bad, we cannot experience the good.

This is why I am sharing my stories with you. I want you to know that I am you, and you are me. We cannot fear who we were born to be. Fear is a great motivator. Fear is also a liar. Let me tell you something: everything you dream of is on the other side of fear. While I still grapple with different fears, I never allow myself to believe that these fears will shape my future. There is nothing better than kicking fear in the face, feeling uncomfortable, and then reaping the benefits of knowing how strong we are.

This is what my "Big Boys" have taught me.

**My Life With The Big Boys** is an anthology of the most influential people in my life. It is raw and gritty. These influencers have not all been positive, but they have been unforgettable lessons. And it is not as glamorous as you may think. The fact is, I allowed people to suck my energy and distract me from my goals. I learned how to own the bad and celebrate the good. I also learned that I do not have time for drama.

*Can you imagine this?*

My wish is that you read my stories, connect with them, and learn that you have the power to create a narrative in your life that is powerful and authentic. After all, there is only one you, and you are special. You have all the tools you need to succeed, even when the chips are stacked against you.

Trust me on this.

**Always remember your voice matters. And always remember you are a star.**

*Xo - Kim D.*

# INTRODUCTION

*"I have no fear, I only have love."*
*- Stevie Nicks*

Ever since I was a little girl, I didn't dream of being a teacher, a nurse, or even an astronaut. No, my heart set its sights on something different. My dream was to be a wife.

Mind you, I knew I would not be an ordinary wife. I would be the best wife in the world. To me, a wife meant being a partner in adventures. A wife offered up a world of possibilities. A wife was the person where her partner laid his head to rest every night.

Being a wife is the noblest profession in the world.

**Picture it:**

I am arranging bouquets of fresh flowers in the kitchen, surrounded by the scent of seasonal candles, while music fills the background. Every night, my handsome husband strolls into the warm embrace of our beautiful home, greeted with a dish of hearty pasta and an ice-cold martini. I yearned for this simple dream of true love, with, of course, the accouterments of a luxurious lifestyle. We would jet set off to exotic locations with our dogs in tow. Our life would be an adventure, and I would be looking fabulous during the entire process. I could see this idyllic life vividly as a little girl. I was confident I could manifest everything I was dreaming of.

**However, as the old saying goes, when we make plans, God laughs.**

Being a wife was my original goal, yet it was not in the cards. As a smart woman, I did have a Plan B. Always have a Plan B, doll, because if you don't, you will be stuck in a situation that will suck the life out of you. Having a Plan B gives you the power to command your life and have an exit plan when things go wrong.

## POSCHE

As you may know, beauty, fashion, and animals are my obsessions. I am obsessed with making sure everything I touch adds a bit of beauty into the world. This is why I got into fashion and opened the iconic boutique Posche. Posche was my savior, my slice of heaven, and an oasis for the fanciest people in the New Jersey area. I knew how to take care of my clients and have every woman who entered my store feel transformed.

After years of curating this upscale boutique in Wayne, New Jersey, I knew it was time for my first fashion show. I poured my heart and soul into every garment that hung on the racks. I knew if I would not wear the clothes, no one else would. I am a purveyor of fashion and wanted everyone who walked into my boutique to feel beautiful when they left.

My business was thriving, and the producers from Bravo TV's hit reality show Real Housewives of New Jersey recognized my relevance. After all, I was dressing the star of the show, Teresa Guidice.

I was prepared to take the next step and take the Posche brand to the next level. I was ready to host the event of all events.

I understood that Posche was more than a store; it was a place to transform the way you feel about yourself. Everyone who was anyone would visit my shop. The rich and famous were drawn to my mecca of fashion, and I knew this. There is power in knowing you are in control of the way people present themselves to the world. I had a sense of confidence in the fashion industry that was unsurpassed. While this sounds like I am bragging, the truth is making women look beautiful is my superpower.

At this point, I asked myself, why not have a fashion show? It was time; the universe was pushing me towards doing something bigger than myself.

Fate intervened, and I was asked to launch a fashion show at the New Jersey Country Club. Without hesitation, I said, "YES, I am ready!" In fact, I was so ready that my Herve Leger dress and my 5-inch stilettos practically jumped out of my closet and said, "Kim, this is your day to shine!"

My parents had been members of the club for years, and I remember Mom's smile when I told her I not only sold out the show, but I oversold the show. Mom beamed with pride and knew her baby girl was ready to take on the world. Mom had been by my side since day one, and I knew she saw my spark since the day I was born.

I know all women want to feel beautiful. If you admit it or not, there is a rush of dopamine when you look into the mirror, dab on a bit of lipstick, and feel good about how you look. I leveraged this desire to feel beautiful, and I built my empire on this need. It is my gift. When a client walks into my shop, I can visualize their potential and create a look that radiates from within. This intrinsic need for women to feel adored is glorified when they meet Kim D. I am not bragging, but I can take any woman, whether she is tall, short, fat, skinny, or even trans, and provide them with the sexiest armor to slay their day.

This is why I had to share my magic on a bigger stage. I knew the Posche catwalk would provide a platform to inspire women around the world.

Let me tell you, Posche was a labor of love. Every single garment in my store called to me. From the asymmetrical hemlines to the curve-hugging bodysuits, I knew women could be transformed by these clothes. Every top, skirt, heel, and necklace is a reflection of Kim D. Every piece of clothing I showcase in Posche is something I need in my closet. Everything about Posche is perfection.

The only problem arises when you invite others into your space who do not have the manners or class to reflect your brand properly.

## ENTER THE MODELS AND THE MESS

I enlisted a few of the girls from RHONJ to strut the catwalk of my inaugural fashion show. You know the show Real Housewives of New Jersey? It is the one I starred on for six seasons. I was portrayed as the instigator of the cast, or even better yet, the villain, because I was determined to keep it real. I made a vow to myself that when I signed on for RHONJ, I was not going to shrink into a wallflower; I would tell the truth whether they liked it or not. If the cast did not agree with my no-nonsense approach, I did not care. What mattered was that Andy Cohen loved it!

**Back to my models.**

These girls are troopers. I asked a few close friends and "Housewives" to model various brands on the catwalk. Without hesitation, I received yes after yes. The run of the show was proving to be star-studded. The Housewives are seasoned reality show stars and know how to take a story to the next level. The fashion show guests would not know what hit them. These beautiful women rallied around me and my dream for a fashion extravaganza. Jacqueline, Teresa, and Danielle were gorgeous guests. Their skin was flawless, their makeup and hair were ready to go, and they knew how to strut their stuff. Per usual, these women showed up to any event lacquered in makeup, drenched in diamonds, and ready to take their heels off and toss them your way.

In the world of Jersey glamour, the kickoff for my fashion show was all about choosing Ashley over Christine. Ashley Holmes, Jacqueline Laurita's daughter, had made her distaste for another castmate, Danielle Staub, quite clear. To be fair, Danielle had gained notoriety for being a villain, but within every villain, there is a charming quality. Don't get me wrong, I adored Christine, Danielle's daughter, but I had reservations about her age. With all the buzz around the event, not to mention the drinking, I thought it might be a bit much for her. As a business owner, sometimes you are forced to make critical decisions and set personal feelings aside. I chose Ashley, a beautiful young woman, and never looked back. This was my maiden voyage into creating a stage for Posche fashion, after all!

I had to navigate it carefully and ensure all the players were aligned.

## The Venue

The North Jersey Country Club, well, that's not just any place, dolls. It's as exclusive as it gets, and only members can host events there. Lucky for me, my mother and stepfather were long-standing members. My mom was beaming with pride when I not only sold an insane number of tickets but I oversold the event! The place was absolutely packed to the rafters.

As I sashayed in, I greeted my stunning models and gave them a pep talk. "You are gorgeous, you are the stars of tonight," I quipped. They were beyond thrilled, knowing they'd be on international TV. After that, I waltzed over to the bar and treated myself to a bottle of Veuve Clicquot champagne – because, why not? We must reward ourselves after hard work.

I meticulously arranged the seating, but when I strolled into the main room, it was like a hurricane hit my plans! The guests were milling around with no direction. My mother, of course, wasn't thrilled. Mom knew a proper seating arrangement was the key to a well-oiled event. Mom scurried around trying to escort our guests to the correct tables.

I was in a tizzy until The Housewives' main producer, the genius Carlos King, decided to take matters into his own hands and rearranged everything. Danielle and Kim G on one side of the catwalk, while Teresa, Jac, and yours truly ended up right across from them. Oh, and did I mention we had to stare at each other all night?

*Can you imagine?*

The confusion was wild, but we managed to sort it out. Danielle Staub, the matriarch of all reality show villains, was always fashionably late. True to Danielle's nature, she held up my show. When Danielle spotted Ashley, she was absolutely livid. She went off on a tirade, calling her all sorts of unsavory names as she strutted down the Posche catwalk. The truth is Danielle had a beef with her that was born on the set of RHONJ. I did not want the reality show drama to spill onto my event. Everything had to be perfect.

Meanwhile, at my table, the spunky 18-year-old Ashley couldn't resist teasing Danielle. She waved at her while Danielle seethed. At some point, I looked around and realized that Teresa had vanished from my table and the room. Teresa is the matriarch of RHONJ, and she commands attention in any room she enters. Her quiet exit was notable to everyone at my event.

Little did I know that Teresa had received a text from the producers, informing her that Danielle had headed to the ladies' room. They told Teresa to take a seat outside so they could have a little chat. Well, that "chat" escalated into a full-blown scream-fest, with Teresa vehemently denying her foreclosure. Danielle poked the bear. And the rest is reality television history.

Jacqueline joined the fray, and the two of them started chasing Danielle through the club, breaking dishes and glasses, terrorizing our guests. It was pure mayhem! And it was pure reality TV gold.

Danielle eventually escaped, with her precious but broken Manolo Blahnik heels in tow. She sought refuge in the bushes, sobbing and unable to walk. Her bodyguard was clearly not cut out for this rowdy crowd, but eventually, he saved her and pulled her out of the bushes. Ashley seized the moment and yanked her weave out!

*You can't make this stuff up!*

All I wanted was to promote fashion to my patrons, and when the Housewives joined, it ceased being about fashion and became all about the drama.

The drama escalated as Danielle called the Wayne police. "This cannot be happening," I thought. When I stepped outside, there were ten cop cars on the scene. They asked Teresa to step into a separate room to have a chat, but she was her usual outspoken self, refusing to cooperate. I intervened and calmed the situation down. "Teresa," I said, "It is all going to be ok, let's talk about this." Teresa's temper got the best of her as she raced after Danielle. I clung to the back of her couture dress as she raced after Danielle. Trust me, Teresa is a force to be reckoned with!

Teresa stormed through the room and the guests were fleeing due to the chaos. It was a frenzy of loud voices and confusion. One of my dearest friends tried to stop Teresa, and she spun her around like a rag doll. My friend exclaimed, "This is f*cking insane!" And that, my dolls, sums it all up! Insanity.

While threads of crazy weave throughout my story, my story is one of strength, outrageous detours from the norm, and understanding my truest self. I have found true love, true friends, and experienced true drama. However, if this Jersey girl can withstand the drama, so can you.

# CHAPTER 1: DOROTHY GRANATELL AND ELVIRA DE PAOLA

*The Ones Who Loved Me From Day One*

*"A girl should be two things: who and what she wants."*
- Coco Chanel

Dorothy Dudek De Paola Miceli Granatell was not only my mother; she was a force to be reckoned with. Mom had a lot of names, but she was my everything. She was just mom to me. Dorothy was the one who taught me the power of femininity. She understood the power of a bold lip and stilettos.

Dorothy gave me the tools to understand my strength as a woman. Mom took pride in how she appeared, and even during her darkest days, she held her head up high. And she never looked back.

Mom grew up dirt poor. When I say dirt poor, I mean she grew up in the bowels of poverty. Mom did not have hot water in her early childhood home and often went to bed hungry. Grandma, while prideful, would have to boil water for Mom to take a bath.

*Can you imagine? No hot water?*

As a child, Mom had a revolving closet of three dresses she would wear to school. This small wardrobe was all her family

1

could afford. Her classmates quickly caught on that she was poor, pointed fingers, and snickered. She was an easy target. She knew her family suffered from financial hardships, and she vowed to herself at an early age that she would never live in the bowels of poverty again.

Mom and me

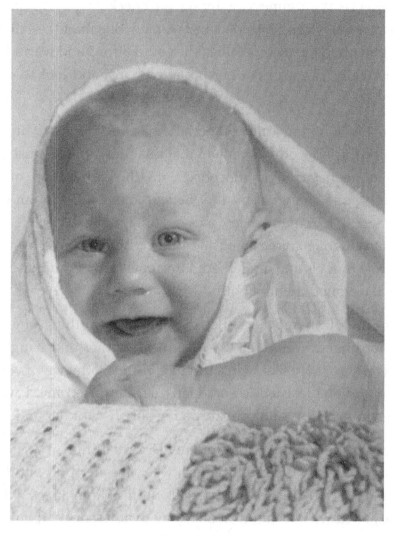

My first photoshoot

When I was born, Mom made sure that I did not want for anything as a child. Dorothy wanted her child to never experience the ugliness of living paycheck to paycheck. She gave me everything I needed and wanted. She made certain her daughter had the nicest clothes she could afford and warm food in her belly. She worked hard, played hard, and looked good doing it.

There is nothing more special than a mother-daughter relationship. Dorothy and I had that relationship. The push and pull of teenage angst morphed into the admiration of the woman who changed my life. Believe me, I was not an easy teenager. I, like many teens, was the antagonist in her life. Yet, Dorothy, while stern, loved me unconditionally. We learn by our role models and are tethered by generational trauma. Mom was the embodiment of both.

Mom and I shared a connection that was nothing short of extraordinary. We weren't your typical mother and daughter; no, we were more like twins, inseparable. Dorothy was a young mom and she learned lessons daily as she raised me. I was a honeymoon baby, and probably a big surprise for her and Dad.

Mom's fashion sense oozed into my DNA naturally. I would sit in Mom's bedroom as a little girl, watching her pull out dress after dress looking for the perfect outfit. Mom knew which shoes went with what outfit and how to accessorize. It was her gift.

My mom was a vision of beauty (in my eyes and most other people's eyes). She was a former Miss Paterson and the first runner-up in the Miss New Jersey pageant. She possessed a talent that could light up a room. Mom would walk into a room, and she made you feel like you were the most important person in the world.

Dorothy had many love affairs in her life. She was on the search for a partner who was her equal and would support a glamorous lifestyle. She knew what she was worth and did not settle for anything less.

Mom and Dad met when she was very young. They were both searching for something. Mom was searching for freedom from poverty, and Dad was looking for a steady companion. For all intents and purposes, Mom and Dad agreed that they hopped quickly into a serious relationship that they were not ready for. They divorced when I was a baby, but remained committed to raising their energetic daughter as a team. They chose to love their child above anything else. Until the day they died, they remained the best of friends.

As I grew, we created a unique family unit. Mind you, this was the seventies, this was before blended families were in vogue. Mom had the instinct to understand that I needed my father in my life. Because Mom emphasized the importance of family, Dad was a part of every momentous occasion in my life.

Holidays were a testament to our unconventional bonds, with both my mother and her husband joining my father and his wife for celebrations. They weren't just cordial; they were genuine friends who supported each other through thick and thin. They'd attend all my fashion shows, sitting at the same table, sharing in my successes. My Dad, in particular, relished the limelight, dancing with the models at my fashion shows and basking in the flashes of the cameras. My mom even made appearances on a few episodes of RHONJ.

*You can't make this stuff up!*

Our life together unfolded in a cozy two-family house in East Paterson, which would later be renamed Elmwood Park. Upstairs, my maternal grandmother held residence, a constant presence throughout my childhood. These two strong women were my anchors. If you need to know anything about me, remember this: I have always surrounded myself with strong women.

My mother was incredibly devoted to her, and I cherished having her close. She was a culinary genius, an easygoing soul who adored my mother and, in turn, loved all her grandchildren. Mom had a sister and three brothers, one of whom was only a couple of years older than me. I spent countless hours with him and my cousins.

Birthdays and holidays were critical in our household. When I say critical, I mean they were the basis for how the women in our family are judged. There was a buzz, a feel, a climax of excitement. Christmas Eve was always an affair to remember, where our family gathered, and, with great anticipation, the kids were allowed to open a single gift. My dad's mother often joined us, and the blend of personalities seemed to mesh effortlessly. Surprisingly, I never thought of our family as broken; it felt whole in its own way.

My mother had a distinct style, and she was certain about how to present her daughter to the world. She kept my hair cut short in a pixie, and my blonde locks were so pale they appeared white. Add to that white lashes and brows, and my low raspy voice, and you couldn't ignore me in a crowd.

Mom was a fashion icon, dressing me in the most stylish and beautiful outfits, with shoes to match every color, while she rocked the latest go-go boots in every shade. I would sit on her bed as she tore through her closet deciding what to wear out to dinner. I was mesmerized by her clothes. There was something magical about how Mom transformed into a glamorous woman right before my eyes.

With her striking red hair and piercing blue eyes, my mother was always surrounded by equally gorgeous friends, and I, little me, would turn heads wherever we went. Mom loved the attention I would get. Her tiny little daughter, with the husky voice, would make an impression wherever she went.

We spent a lot of time in Florida, traveling with my mother's divorced friends and their children. As a young girl, I loathed flying; the motion sickness and ear pain were relentless. However, once we touched down in the Sunshine State, the good times rolled. Fabulous dinners, adorned in the cutest outfits, promised the most fun a little girl could ever dream about. I even had the opportunity to see Donny Osmond and his brothers perform live. Donny sang directly to me once, a moment I captured in a photograph.

*Oh, I still love Donny. I am still in puppy love.*

Weekends were a time for my father's mother, Elvira, who lived in a charming white house on Mary Street in Paterson, NJ. The neighborhood was punctuated by a beautiful church on one corner and, on the other, our family's bar, The J & J, named after my grandfather and his brother, John and Joe. My grandmother managed the bar during the day, and my father transformed it into a nightclub by night. I practically grew up in that bar, where my grandmother spoiled me with everything I could ever want. At one point, I even had three dogs and a cat, who decided to give birth right on top of me in the middle of the night, gifting me with six kittens. There was nothing more magical for me at the moment than holding six newborn kittens in my arms. Grandma smiled and left me to myself. She knew my love for animals would guide me through the experience. My grandmother was unshakably calm and patient; she was an embodiment of love.

My paternal grandfather adored me just as much. Our nights were filled with bonding over episodes of Johnny Carson, the late-night host. Many nights, I would fall asleep by the dim glow of the Zenith TV.

My grandmother was a whiz in the kitchen, and she could whip up incredible dishes using a single black wrought-iron pan. Her porterhouse steak remains etched in my memory. She had the God-given talent to perfect the steak with a seared crust on the outside and a buttery flavor that melts in your mouth.

Dad would make occasional appearances while I visited, living a playboy lifestyle, staying up late and sleeping in. Dad was a night owl, and every moment he was not working, he would make every effort to squeeze in some daddy/daughter time.

Daddy had a lot of girlfriends but always included me in his adventures. If I did not approve of his latest love interest, he would not date her.

My favorite among his women-friends was named Marianne, who had the most beautiful German Shepherd, Raja. I was utterly obsessed with him, and the feeling was mutual. I snuggled up to Raja as dad and Marianne went about their day.

Dad did his best to parent me, and I never felt that I was missing out on the father-daughter relationship.

My dad and his friends doted on me, but I always returned to my grandmother's care at night. Grandma and grandpa were surrogate parents; I always felt safe and adored in their home. My grandparents filled the gaps when my parents were pulled in other directions.

As for my mother, her life took her on the road frequently, and I would spend weeks or even a month without her. Mom was a jetsetter, and I enjoyed watching every moment of her life. Her life felt glamorous.

When she was home, mom was present. She'd drive me to school at St. Leo's in Elmwood Park. It was there that she shared stories from my early years, ones that hinted at my lifelong connection with animals. We'd visit petting zoos, and the animals seemed to gravitate toward me, particularly the lambs, who became despondent when I left. My love for animals continued to grow, but my mother, busy with her travels, didn't allow pets in our lives. This made my grandmother's home a sanctuary for me, a place where I could be close to animals and feel at ease.

You might be wondering, how does my grandmother fit into the story of my life as a Jersey girl? My grandmother was a formidable woman who was always on the go. This was an era when women were tethered to the home and their children. Women rarely worked. However, grandma ran several businesses and raised a family. She raised her two sons almost single-handedly while my grandfather, a charming but roguish character, pursued his own interests.

*You know what I mean.*

She put my uncle through college, and together, they ventured into real estate investments. My grandmother always dressed impeccably, wearing smart dresses and low heels every day.

Grandma's name was Elvira. My father initially wanted to name me after her, but my mother swiftly vetoed that idea. Thus, Kimberlee it was. She loved my grandmother but had a different vision for my name.

Watching my grandmother in action was inspiring. She hustled and worked hard, showing me the power of determination and grit. My godfather (my uncle) even remarked that I was quite like her in many ways, except when it came to men.

As a child at my grandmother's house, discipline was a foreign concept. I never got spanked or the belt; instead, I was encouraged to speak and express myself. There was only one incident when my father raised his voice to me, and it was because I had inadvertently tripped my grandmother while walking one of my dogs. She fell, and my father chastised me for being careless. My grandmother, with her unshakeable composure, assured everyone that it was an accident, and that was the first and last time my father ever yelled at me.

Life with my grandmother was pure fun. She took us to visit her relatives, and I loved mingling with the adults, who all admired her. She was fiercely proud of her Italian heritage, speaking with a strong Sicilian accent. She'd ask everyone she met, "Are you Italian?" and if they answered yes, she'd inquire further, searching for connections to Sicily. If they weren't of Sicilian descent, she'd dismiss them, stating, "No, they're not Italian." She was a character, no doubt, deeply rooted in her Sicilian heritage.

Rules were loose in my household. I was allowed to stay up watching Johnny Carson. This may be concerning to some parents, especially when I had to wake up early for school in another town. My grandmother had an anecdote to my late nights as she would provide warm washcloths on my forehead to wake me from my sleep. It wasn't easy, but I managed to make it to school.

"Kimberlee," Grandma would whisper, "It's time to rise and shine". Her voice was comforting and I knew I could do anything with her by my side.

School is everything. However, it was not everything in the De Paola household. We held experiences as an important part of our education.

The bar during the day was my playground. My grandmother would engage in conversations with the regulars, cashing their checks and serving them drinks. She knew each of their stories, and these stories were important to her. She managed the entire establishment, not as a bartender, but as a master of ceremonies. My adolescence was filled with tales from my grandmother and adventures with my friends. She drove us everywhere, despite her diminutive stature and her beloved Pekingese dog, whose breath made the car slightly pungent. We didn't mind; we had our freedom and she was our beloved chauffeur.

## MOM MEETS DAD

Mom got married to my dad at a very young age. She was unsure of herself, but the one thing she was sure of is that she wanted to escape the poverty she was born into. Their love was fleeting and it was a nod to the innocence of the day, where everyone was expected to be married and have kids by the age of 21. They met those expectations, yet were never really ready to commit for the rest of their lives. I never felt abandoned or in the middle of a tug-of-war as a child. My parents were friends and committed to raising their daughter.

Returning to my father's life, one particular girlfriend, Marianne, and her dog Raja, left a lasting mark on me. My love for fur babies was ignited at a very young age. Raja was my very special friend. I spent countless hours at the back of the bar, teaching Raja tricks and playing shuffleboard. The backdrop of countless hours with Raja was accompanied by the jukebox, a source of endless entertainment. Though I was often the only child around, I was content, as my furry friends kept me company, and I enjoyed mingling with the adults.

And so, my early years as a Jersey girl were painted with the colorful characters of my family, each playing a unique role in my life, teaching me essential lessons along the way. Each adult in my life played a special role. However, the one constant was Dorothy. She was my rock.

Mom was with me from the very beginning of my Housewives journey. She enjoyed watching her oldest daughter on camera and even joined me in some episodes. Funny thing, she was tickled when she saw me entangled in the curse-filled banter. Can you imagine that? Dorothy encouraged me to be myself — warts and all. When my face was tear-stained after a dramatic row, she would say, "Kim, you are a De Paola, you are full of fire and wit — no one can extinguish this from you".

*Thank you, mom. Lesson learned.*

## JERSEY FLASHBACK

The Birth of Posche and My Reality TV Journey

My love for my mother's wardrobe as a little girl blossomed into a passion for fashion as an adult. Watching Dorothy meticulously pick out the perfect outfit for any occasion inspired my career goals. I wanted to help all women look and feel their absolute best, welcoming all shapes and sizes. In August 2008, my baby, Posche by Kim D., opened in Wayne, NJ. It was a 500-square-foot venue, a true diamond in the rough, offering the most glamorous clothing to the elite women of Jersey.

This is where I met and befriended Jacqueline, Teresa, and the cameras. I remember the first time the cameras came into Posche — it was thrilling! Everywhere you looked in the store, there was a camera. The producers blocked out the windows and doors — it was the real deal.

They were set up to film on international TV! My little boutique, Posche, made it to international TV. It was a dream come true.

Jacqueline and Teresa came to shop at my boutique, and I was so excited that I went above and beyond for them. I had orange juice and the best champagne on ice to serve the girls mimosas. When they walked in, I handed both girls a mimosa. Teresa's glass said "diva" on one side, which I felt was so her! I still have those fabulous glasses I served them with to this day.

Filming with the girls was a blast. The cameras loved our authenticity. We were friends on and off camera — the kind of friends who would dine at upscale restaurants or make the best of seemingly boring tasks together.

After filming at Posche for the first time, the three of us went to a local restaurant with a friend. I remember having a conversation with Teresa about Joe, her husband at the time. She asked what I would do if I thought my husband was cheating on me. I immediately told her I would hire a private investigator to find out the truth. Jacqueline did not agree with my approach, and the topic was not brought up again.

If we weren't in Posche or at the best restaurants in the area, we were talking on the phone for hours. I recall being on the phone with Teresa while she folded her clothes until 1:30 a.m. We loved staying up late talking, but we preferred our times in local upscale restaurants.

At the time, we would film at the best restaurants, and everything we ate and drank was always comped! The restaurants loved having us. We were great company, and the press was huge.

We all shared the same zodiac sign—we're Tauruses. The Taurus star sign is ruled by the persistent and determined Bull. When it comes to their energy, the typical Taurus person has two speeds: relaxed and contented (picture them grazing in a green pasture) or hyped-up and ready to charge. Do you understand us now? The three of us truly had so much fun together, and the producers captured it flawlessly.

The first experience with the cameras felt intensely close to my face. If you know me, it's not surprising that I loved it! I felt right at home with every camera. I never thought of acting in any way other than being Kim D.

I was myself, always true to my nature. Most of the time, when the cameras were rolling, I wouldn't pay any attention to them. I knew immediately my next great adventure in life would involve the cameras. All my life, I've always gone headfirst into everything I did.

I attribute this to my mother, Dorothy, and my grandmother, Elvira. I never settled for 'good enough' in my life. I strived for bigger and better. I knew I deserved more and would have more, with determination and grit my grandmother handed down to me. I knew I was unstoppable and could pursue any adventure I set my mind to with my mother's support in tow.

This is how the second Posche by Kim D., bigger and better, came to fruition. A 1500-square-foot boutique in Allendale, NJ, opened in 2015. Staying where I started wasn't an option—I had to move on. I had to make my dynamic duo proud. Dorothy's support and Elvira's strength made me fearless.

## MORAL OF THE STORY

Don't forget where you came from, and know who believed in you from day one.

In life's unpredictable journey, there's a profound lesson echoing through the corridors of time: never forget your roots and the unwavering support of those who believed in you from the outset. It's a mantra that resonates with undeniable truth, reminding us to honor our origins and the individuals who stood by us through thick and thin. Whether scaling the dizzying heights of success or weathering the storms of challenges, remembering our humble beginnings and the steadfast champions who cheered us on empowers us with humility, gratitude, and resilience. For it is in acknowledging our past and the unwavering faith of our earliest believers that we find the strength to navigate the complexities of our present and shape the contours of our future.

Me and Dad

#  CHAPTER 2: GUSSY

*The One Who Was My Rock*

> *"A man that doesn't spend time with his family can*
> *never be a real man."*
> -Don Corelone, The Godfather

My life started in the midst of drama.
*Can you imagine?*
Mom married at 21, and less than a year later, she found out she was pregnant with me. Her unorthodox lifestyle, coupled with her youth, was the springboard for exploration. Or more simply put, Mom was unhappy with Dad and had a boyfriend or two.

Before you judge, read on.

Months after Mom and my dad, Gussy De Paola, married, she got dolled up and headed out on the town with a boyfriend. Unfortunately, while headed home, Mom's car was hit head-on, resulting in a crushed ankle. She was whisked off to the hospital as paramedics tried to soothe her cries.

The pain was excruciating as she lay in the hospital bed, and the news she received was even more shocking. Dorothy was unprepared for what her doctor revealed.

Before you make assumptions about Dorothy, know that Dad was working late nights at the bar and had checked out early in their marriage. Mom and Dad tried to make a go of it. They were in love with the idea of being in love. In retrospect, she married Gussy because she wanted to escape the immense poverty she was born into. The home she was raised in did not offer any modern conveniences. She often lay in bed at night hungry, not knowing when her next hot meal would come. Mom and Dad both regretted their hasty decision to marry and remained dear friends for the rest of their lives.

As soon as Mom was settled in her hospital bed, she leaned over and rang Dad on the phone. Her agony was palpable.

"Gussy, I got in a car accident. Can you come to the hospital?" Dad rushed over to Mom's bedside and was greeted by a doctor. The doctor, cloaked in a starched white coat, peered over his clipboard. As he pored over the results, he began to smile.

"Hmmmm," the doctor began as he scanned the papers on the clipboard.

"Dorothy, I have good news for you," the doctor smiled. "You are pregnant." Dad, who was very well aware of Mom's extracurricular activities, grabbed Mom's hand and gave her a kiss on the cheek.

"Dorothy," Dad comforted, "We are going to be parents!" His joy was evident. She lay in the hospital bed, suffering from excruciating pain, and clutched her belly.

"Yes, Gussy, you are going to be a daddy."

**And the rest is history.**

Gussy and Dorothy De Paola filed for divorce before my first birthday. I have no memory of my original family being intact, but I have rich memories of my parents' excellent co-parenting style. Remember, this was the sixties, before co-parenting was even a buzzword.

Dad and Mom would spend holidays together; they supported me in every aspect. The only difference between my family and the rest of the world's was that Mom and Dad were not married. I believe I had a more functional family than most families today. I had love and two parents who respected each other. Most families today do everything they can to mask their dysfunction. Not the De Paolas. The De Paolas are proud of their different way of navigating life.

Dorothy was saddled with a rambunctious toddler. I was precocious, curious, and full of energy. While Mom balanced her life with me, she was also a hot commodity. She was young, gorgeous, and men fell at her feet. She caught the eye of suitors with ease. While Mom dated, I was scooped up by my grandmother, whom I adored. I was raised in a world of strong women.

My weekends were a delightful escape into the indulgent world of my paternal grandmother, Elvira. Elvira resided in a spacious white house on Mary Street in Paterson, NJ. The house stood between a charming church and a family-owned establishment named The J and J, a bar co-founded by my grandfather and his brothers, John and Joe.

Grandma De Paola was a remarkable woman, managing the bar by day and transforming it into a nightclub under my father's care by night. I cherished my time there, surrounded by her unwavering love and indulgence. She granted my every wish, including the companionship of three dogs and a cat, which, incidentally, gave birth to kittens right in my presence one memorable night. The miracle of seeing these little kittens excited me. I was obsessed.

Grandma's composure during unexpected events mirrored her calm and patient demeanor. She possessed a special grace, showering me with affection alongside my grandfather, creating a haven for me. Nights were spent with them, gathered around the television, watching Johnny Carson. Her culinary magic unfolded in a single black wrought-iron pan, with Porterhouse steak being her standout recipe.

While my father led a lively, late-night lifestyle, my grandmother provided stability and warmth. I occasionally joined Dad on outings, particularly relishing the time spent with his girlfriend Marianne and her beloved German Shepherd, Raja. Dogs are everything to me. (Currently, I have eight fur babies).

Despite the occasional rendezvous with my father, my sanctuary was at my grandma's house. She offered solace during my mother's frequent travels, introducing me to a world of petting zoos that incited my special connection with animals. I was transfixed by these exotic creatures. I would ask Grandma if I could have a zebra as a pet. She patted my head, smiled, and ushered me along to the next exhibit.

My grandmother, a trailblazer of her time, ran multiple businesses and played a pivotal role in raising her two sons largely on her own. Despite her husband's carefree ways, she remained devoted, managing finances and investing in real estate. Grandpa was a man about town, and Grandma held down the fort.

Her elegant attire and strong presence reflected her determined spirit. She was always there for me and my curious ways, leaving an incredible mark on my upbringing. Elvira was my hero. I had an inkling that one day I would not only be the best wife, but I would also be a businesswoman, just like her.

Discipline was a rarity at my grandmother's house. When Gussy came into the home and scolded me for my behavior, I had an ally in Grandma. Grandma De Paola diffused his stern words with stoic strength. She understood my situation and wanted me to have idyllic memories. My childhood with her was filled with joy, visits to relatives, and a deep connection to our Italian heritage, particularly her Sicilian roots.

Grandma knew I loved to be entertained and allowed me to stay up late to watch Johnny Carson. The transition from late-night TV to early morning school rides was facilitated by her tender wake-up calls with a warm washcloth.

"Kimberlee," she said with quiet authority, "Kimberlee, it is time for school." Grandma would rub my head, feed me breakfast, and usher me to my elementary school.

Memories of days in the bar, watching her effortlessly manage the patrons, remain vivid, as does the freedom of adolescence spent exploring with friends, chauffeured by her in a car with a small Pekingese. Despite the occasional peculiar odor in her car and the limitations of her vision over the steering wheel, my grandmother's company and adventures were unparalleled. We were like Thelma and Louise. Nothing scared her, and she was always up for impromptu adventures.

Even in the bar's solitude, with no other children around, I found solace in the company of animals and the camaraderie of adults. This is how I grew to be a natural orator. I sat on the floor of the bar, playing with my animals and soaking up all the wisdom of the patrons. I learned to listen and discern fact from fiction.

By the time I was four years old, Mom found Butchie (more to come), her second husband. Mom was swept off her feet by this suave gentleman. He was kind to her daughter and showered us with expensive gifts. She fell for him, no questions asked. I don't recall the first time I met Butch, but I know how he made me feel. He made me feel like a daughter. He made me feel like a princess. He protected me.

I was peeled away from the watchful eye of Elvira, and Mom planned to move in with her new husband. We were excited to become a stable family unit with Butchie.

*Oh boy, we didn't know what we were in for!*

## JERSEY FLASHBACK

### Flashback: First Night of Filming

It was the first night of filming after I officially signed my contract with RHONJ. I found myself thrust into the limelight, facing off against my friend Teresa and her husband Joe. The venue was Capitale on the lower east side, a first-class event where Teresa was being honored for her work with the NephCure Foundation.

I remember vividly the outfit I chose for the occasion: a taupe Victoria Beckham midi dress, complemented by a white Fendi floor-length coat and YSL tribtoos. With a fresh layered haircut, I felt flawless as the cameras began to roll.

Seated at a table with Teresa, Joe, and two other couples, I was suddenly tapped on the shoulder. The producers pulled me aside, hoping I would confirm the rumors circulating about Joe's fidelity. Perez Hilton had just dropped a story insinuating that Joe was cheating on Teresa.

They wanted me to return to the table and announce to Teresa that her husband was being unfaithful. Despite their insistence, I refused to take the bait. I stood firm, knowing I had just signed my contract and feeling confident in my intuition about Joe's character.

After Teresa's speech, I discreetly gathered all the girls and suggested we head to the bar. Teresa and I were close, often exchanging texts at events. Despite multiple failed attempts to alert her under the table, I finally pulled her aside one-on-one.

I wanted to ensure she wasn't blindsided by the rumors swirling around her marriage. Confirming my intuition, I asked if everything was okay between her and Joe. Teresa assured me that it was, dismissing the Perez Hilton allegations as baseless.

Signing the RHONJ contract, I knew I had to do things my way. I refused to be manipulated by the producers and turn my back on my friends, especially when it involved false accusations against a good man. It was against my morals, and it wouldn't be the last time I clashed with the producers over it.

## MORAL OF THE STORY

**Don't judge lest ye be judged.**

The age-old adage, "Don't judge unless you be judged," encapsulates a profound lesson that transcends time and cultural boundaries. At its core lies the recognition of our inherent fallibility and the understanding that passing judgment without full comprehension can lead to unfairness, misunderstanding, and even harm.

In a world brimming with diversity and complexity, it's easy to succumb to snap judgments based on superficial appearances, hearsay, or preconceived notions. Yet, beneath every surface lies a rich tapestry of experiences, struggles, and aspirations that shape an individual's journey. To judge hastily is to deny oneself the opportunity to explore the depths of human complexity and to appreciate the nuances of individual stories.

The act of judgment often reflects more about the one passing judgment than the subject being judged. It reveals biases, insecurities, and limited perspectives that hinder genuine empathy and connection. By exercising restraint in passing judgment, we open ourselves to a world of understanding, empathy, and compassion.

Embracing the lesson of "Don't judge unless you be judged" invites us to approach others with an open heart and a curious mind. It urges us to seek understanding before drawing conclusions, to offer empathy instead of condemnation, and to recognize the inherent dignity and worth of every individual.

In practicing this principle, we not only cultivate a culture of kindness and inclusivity but also embark on a journey of personal growth and enlightenment. For it is in withholding judgment that we create space for meaningful connections, foster mutual respect, and forge bonds that transcend the boundaries of prejudice and bias.

Mom, Butchie and Me

#  CHAPTER 3: BUTCHIE

*The One Who Showed Me A New Life*

> *Do not judge me by my success, judge me by how many*
> *times I fell down and got back up again.*
> — *Nelson Mandela*

FRANK "BUTCH" MICELLI was a thoughtful, generous, caring man who became the cornerstone of my life the day he entered it at 4 years old. I was Butchie's sidekick during the day. As long as the sun was up, I was next to him. Until the day my mom had to exit this relationship, I was his pride and joy. Looking back, I spent much of my formative years next to Frank "Butch" Micelli, my stepfather and notorious mob assassin.

***Yes, I said mob assassin.***

As a kid, Butchie was all about idolizing mobsters. He was fascinated by the underworld and obsessed with trying to walk in their shoes. His parents, easygoing as they were, never called him out on his tall tales. Butchie's mom was a well-known judge and relegated his fascination to just a phase. His antics began at an early age as Butchie was a wheeler and dealer. He leaned on pals at the Social Security office to set up a tracing outfit, sniffing out those who stiffed the neighborhood bookies. He knew he could be an enforcer at a very young age.

In the early '60s, Butchie packed up for Jersey and slid into the driver's seat as the infamous mobster Joseph Paterno's go-to guy. He played the role of enforcer and chauffeured like a boss. His fascination with the mob grew into a reality.

In the 1960s and 1970s, The Paterno Crew, led by the formidable capo Joseph "Don" Paterno, was the muscle for Carlo Gambino's operations in Newark, New Jersey. They were the go-to guys for all the dirty work, raking in hefty profits along the way. This crew of contract killers was notorious for thriving in the midst of various other mob factions, operating in what some call the most corrupt era in American history. They held court as New Jersey's top crime syndicate, dabbling in everything from loan sharking and gambling to truck hijacking and armed robberies. Their repertoire included extortion, assault, and even murder, making them a force to be reckoned with in the underworld.

Butchie's life was all about dodging danger and spinning tall tales. He was in a constant dance between who was a friend and who was an enemy.

Vincent Teresa, another wise guy, saw Butchie as his sworn enemy. In Teresa's book, "My Life in the Mafia," he spills the tea about their clashes and how their lives were tangled up.

Butchie had a fantastic operation going. Their squad had ten men in it, and they got a regular five hundred bucks a week, but that was only a fraction of what they made. They had the best counterfeit business going in the country. There wasn't anything Miceli and his gang couldn't provide. They printed phoney postage stamps, passports, driver's licenses, stock certificates, and cash like it was confetti. New Jersey is the biggest center of counterfeiting in the country. Not only that, but in New Jersey you could buy just about any kind of gun you wanted from Miceli's group: machine guns, hand grenades, mines. I think he could have supplied you with a tank if you needed it.

**-Vincent Teresa, My Life in The Mafia**

Frank "Butch" Miceli is one of those characters you can't help but be drawn to in the mob scene. He left behind a legacy of intrigue and mystique that still keeps folks talking. Yet, to me, he was just my stepdad.

## Butchie and Me

Butchie has been in my life for as long as I can remember. Mom married him when I was four years old. He would scoop me up in his arms and lavish love and gifts all over me. I was so happy every time Butchie walked through the door and gave his girls the biggest hugs.

He was my protector.

I felt safe with Butchie. However, the truth is not all people felt safe in his presence. My stepfather was widely known as the assassin for the mob. His job was to take people out. His profession took him to the seediest corners of the world.

While he lived a duplicitous life, he was the guy who would prove himself to be a constant father figure in my life. He was the one who would wipe my tears from my face and tell me everything would be okay. He treated me like a princess, not a baby. He never made me feel like an outsider.

I fostered much of my ability to "run with the big boys" during my time with Butchie. He instilled in me the strength to stand my ground and to be generous. Butchie also included me in everything he and mom did. He would bring me to the Copacabana, where I would entertain his friends with songs and dance. Yes, the Copa.

In the vibrant heart of New York City, amidst the neon-lit streets and the rhythm of jazz, stood the legendary Copacabana. It wasn't just a nightclub; it was a center of glamour, pulsating with life and hedonism, the epicenter of the city's nightlife during the swinging '60s and '70s.

At the center of it all was the dance floor, a whirlwind of movement and passion. Couples twirled and dipped to the rhythm of the music, their laughter mingling with the sounds of clinking glasses and applause. Celebrities rubbed shoulders with mobsters, politicians with socialites, all united by their love for the extravagant lifestyle that the Copacabana offered. And I sat center stage, lapping it all in.

I know what you're thinking, how old was Kim at the Copa Cabana?!

*What the... what the?*

That's right, I was four years old hanging out with the big boys. What can I say, it was my playground! And I loved it. The Copa was vibrant, exciting, and had indescribable energy. I would sit there, sipping on a Kiddie Cocktail, watching the fanciest people on earth hobnob with my parents. Frank Sinatra would stop by and grab Butchie by the arm, giving him a big kiss on the cheek.

I learned to capture the attention of adults at a very early age. I would sit within earshot of adult conversations and absorb every detail. Primarily, the tone, mannerisms, and grit of these powerful men intrigued me. Although I was young, I wasn't looked at as an inconvenience. I was welcomed into the world of Butchie. I didn't know it at the time, but I was preparing for my life ahead. I was setting the stage by strengthening my sense of self.

In my mind, Butchie embodied the essence of generosity and integrity. He was the kind of man who would notice a need and fulfill it without being asked. His arms would be filled with beautiful gifts, treats, and decor for the home. He would show up time and time again as the same man in all situations he ran in.

**Picture this:**

Butchie drives Patti (my cousin) home and notices her family's apartment does not have an air conditioner. He had an empathetic nature toward those he loved. Without saying a word, Frank buys an air conditioner and has it delivered to the home the following day.

Butchie would buy me insane clothing. I know he was the first big boy to give me a taste of luxury. Money was no limit. Money flowed from Butchie's pockets, and we were the beneficiaries.

Butchie purchased the most stunning dresses. I felt like a princess in the clothes he would buy on our shopping trips. Anything I wished for would be purchased by my stepfather. Dresses, clothes, toys, and more flooded in like a tsunami. Mind you, everything I wore was top of the line. Butchie's girls would not be seen in tacky dress-up clothes. Mom and I were an extension of Butchie's brand. We wore elegant, high-end fashion pieces that mirrored his taste. After all, if we did not look good, he did not look good.

**His fashion sense left an impression on me to this day.**

He wasn't the kind of guy to give you his shirt off his back; he'd buy you your own shirt. If he looked good, he wanted you to look good. Partly because he wanted to make sure you had the best, partly because he dressed to the nines. Butchie was undoubtedly the best-dressed person in any crowd.

Butchie was very particular about almost everything. He even took pride in his monogrammed boxer shorts. Mom would spend countless hours over the ironing board getting the crease perfect in his undershorts.

He demanded perfection. I can still picture how the heads in a room would turn the moment Butchie walked in. I'm serious when I say all eyes were on Butchie wherever we were.

Even Butchie's mugshot tells the story of his love for fashion. Yes, Butchie had legal troubles and eventually spent time in prison. However, he knew how to present himself to the world no matter what his situation.

When Butchie was arrested, he did it in style. He wore a red sports jacket, perfectly pressed against the backdrop of the police headquarters. Butchie was a palpable force in more ways than one.

His house was decorated with tasteful yet gaudy pieces. I use the word "gaudy" in a favorable manner. Gaudy was the style of the day. Butchie searched high and low for statement pieces that would make his guests stop and stare.

Ornate and over-the-top was what he loved. Oversized mahogany furniture with inlaid gold was his style. He chose decor that was the best of the best, making a statement that Butchie had money. It was all about appearances with Butchie.

This was a man with a phone in his bathroom. It wasn't normal to be on the phone in the bathroom at this time. He wanted to stand out and be known as a man who commanded respect. Can you imagine Butchie on the "throne" while wheeling and dealing with his guys?

When people would ask him what he did for a job, he would respond "milkman" with a sly grin. No one needed to know what he did for a living, not even mom.

Butchie was a man of high taste, from his clothes to his dinners. My mom made dinner every night at 5 P.M. without fail. No leftovers for Butchie. That was mom's job to please her husband. She bent over backwards trying to be the perfect housewife, unaware of his dark profession.

Presenting his family first was the focus as you entered his home. Every space on the walls was peppered with pictures of his growing family. We are talking about extended family members too. Every family member had a special space on Butchie's wall.

He was constantly hosting large family gatherings at the house, grilling over 150 chicken cutlets at a given holiday gathering. Butchie always offered the best of the best for everyone in his life. His generosity was contagious.

He took care of all the kids. Butchie put an in-ground pool right off the house with an impeccable backyard. The man's good taste extended into his hosting spaces. He would host everyone and anyone in his circle in that backyard, swimming, cooking, drinking, dancing. A luxury few had at the time. I was blissfully unaware of how he made his money to afford these luxuries. I was young and carefree; it was a blessing as I was ignorant of his mob affiliation.

Butchie's style and charisma would leave a lasting impression on everyone in his presence. He was a guy of the people. He often had parties inviting the whole family. When I say family, I mean his relatives, our relatives, the neighbors — everyone we knew coming together to eat delicious food, expensive drinks, and host the most insane 4th of July parties that were the highlight of the neighborhood each year. Backyard BBQs around the pool like you wouldn't believe!

I felt safe and secure in who I was growing up under Butchie's wing. I was safe to be who I was in every situation I entered. I knew kids at school weren't going to mess with me because I was 'mobbed up'. I had the toughest man I knew in my corner caring, loving, and developing the mentality I would later rely on. I didn't recognize it at the time, but Butchie helped form the Kim D. persona you know and love.

One day stands out in my mind, that made me question Butchie for a split second. This was the day that the FBI raided our home. As you can imagine, the shock that penetrated my mom, cousin Patti, and myself in the morning when the FBI barged into our home accusing him of robbery.

"FBI, OPEN UP!" The echo of their forceful entry into our home is something I will never forget.

"Butchie could never do anything like this," I thought. "The FBI must be at the wrong house." My heart raced. I did not have an inkling into his secret life.

Mom patted me on the head and soothed my heightened anxiety. "Kim," Mom consoled, "Everything will be fine. You know Butchie, and he is not a troublemaker."

The contrast between the allegations we heard and the man we knew had us grappling with disbelief and confusion. They did not find Butchie in the house that morning. Butchie was always one step ahead of the Feds, and he snuck into the basement after they left.

When I was young, Mom and Butchie would leave me with a trusted protector. I loved this guy, Alex. We would spend hours playing in the pool, eating ice cream, and playing hide and go seek. Alex was the person who taught me how to swim. I came to look forward to my time when my parents would leave, and I would have time with Alex. Alex was my protector and my best playmate. Unfortunately, this would not be the case for a long time.

I grew up in a Catholic home, and the rite of religious passage for any Catholic is their communion into the church. Mom was busy preparing the meal for my illustrious indoctrination into the church. She pulled out all her culinary tricks, from chicken cutlets, pasta, and even replicated Butchie's mother's famous cannolis. Butchie's mother was not only a fabulous chef; she was a judge by day. During the final preparation of my big event, Mom's ears were on high alert.

This, of all days, was the moment Mom's eyes were wide open. And she did not like what she heard one bit. Mom was a people pleaser and never liked to rock the boat. She loved Butchie and wanted their marriage to be successful.

Remember, Mom did not know exactly what Butchie did for a living. She knew he was "connected," but she didn't ask questions. He was suave, charismatic, and had a way of diffusing Mom's inquiries.

However, on the day of my communion, Mom overheard Butchie talking to one of his guys. Butchie was soft-spoken but clear in his message. He was a champion for Alex. His guys were adamant. "You guys, Alex is no threat, no action needs to be taken."

What did he mean by no action? What was Butchie talking about? All the dots were connected for Mom. She had a difficult time processing the fact that the man she loved was involved in sinister acts.

Alex met a fate that was brutal and quick. My beloved babysitter was never to be seen again. Mom heard it all. Mom was no dummy, and these words sealed the end of their marriage. When Mom heard these words, her world became dark and dizzy. Dorothy went into a space that was unrelenting, which needed immediate medical attention. Mom passed out on the day of my communion and was whisked away to the hospital for care. How could she be married to this man for so long and not know his devious ways? Her panic and anxiety overtook her, and she needed respite.

*Then she needed a divorce.*

My mom wanted out of her second marriage, and that's when Butchie dropped the family, no longer taking care of everyone. Mom packed our things and left Butchie, never to look back. It takes courage to walk away from everything you know. Her strength was evident when she went toe to toe with one of the most dangerous men in the mob.

Our story does not end there. I had an inkling of Butchie's nefarious ways, but I never saw him as evil. I became close to Butchie as an adult. Even after Butchie and Mom split, I would visit him in Florida. He always considered me family, as I considered him a father figure. He was just my stepfather, and my blissful ignorance allowed me to compartmentalize him as such. Butchie was a master of feeding us lies, myths sprinkled with a little truth.

Butchie was misdiagnosed with multiple sclerosis for ten years. It turns out that he had a tumor growing on his spine. In his later years, after serving 9 years in prison, he became widely known as the "crippled mobster". To many, he was smug and arrogant. However, his family always rallied around him. Even his mother, the judge, to her dying day, believed in his innocence.

From The New York Times, June 14th, 1977:

HACKENSACK, June 13 — Frank Miceli, an alleged lieutenant in the crime "family" of the late Carlo Gambino, pleaded guilty today to nine bribery and conspiracy charges stemming from an 11-month investigation of loan-sharking and other illicit activities in 1974 and 1975.

Mr. Miceli, who has been described by law enforcement authorities as the No. 2 man in North Jersey rackets, had been ordered on June 1 to stand trial on Sept. 12. Judge Morris Malech of Superior Court had rejected an appeal that his case be placed on an inactive list because the 42-year-old defendant suffers from multiple sclerosis and is physically unable to withstand a trial.

Me and The Supremes

## JERSEY FLASHBACK

Son Cubano

As the day began, Teresa and I made our way to the salon to get ready for my Posche fashion show. The atmosphere was buzzing with excitement, and we were greeted by a guy named Angelo who seemed eager to assist us. He even offered us champagne, adding a touch of luxury to our salon experience.

But things took an unexpected turn when Angelo started chatting with Teresa about Melissa Gorga, mentioning how she had danced at the club he managed. Teresa's reaction was priceless - she seemed on the verge of falling off her chair at the mere mention of Melissa. I couldn't help but find the whole situation comical.

After our salon visit, we headed to my show at Son Cubano, a sleek and seductive restaurant. I had a feeling drama was brewing, but little did I know just how intense it would become. It turned out that Melissa recognized Angelo right away, and tensions quickly escalated.

Unbeknownst to me, Teresa and Melissa were filming a scene in the ladies' room about the salon encounter. Melissa even called her husband Joe, who promptly flew down to the restaurant with Ritchie Wachile'. On the way, Ritchie tried to calm Joe down, but the situation was already spiraling out of control.

Suddenly, the producers approached me and insisted I go outside to film. Confused, I followed their instructions, only to be met with screams and profanities. To my shock, Joe Gorga was directing his anger towards me, and I wasted no time firing back.

In the midst of the chaos, Joe raised his fist towards me, but Melissa intervened just in time. I stood my ground, telling Joe, "You are nothing! You are a midget! I play with the big boys!" asserting my authority over my own show. It was a moment of defiance that ultimately earned me a paid contract with Bravo and a spot as a friend of the next season.

Meanwhile, inside the restaurant, my son was trying to come to my defense, but the producers held him back. When I returned, I was filled with adrenaline and disgust, but I knew I had to keep the show going for my paying guests. So, I grabbed the mic and rallied the crowd, urging them to stay and enjoy the evening despite the drama.

Looking back, I still can't believe that such behavior was tolerated, but it was a defining moment that shaped my journey in the world of reality TV.

## MORAL OF THE STORY

Do not judge a book by its cover. Behind every relationship lies a story.

Much like a book's cover, which may offer only a glimpse of the story within, a person's appearance, background, or initial demeanor can only reveal a fraction of who they truly are. Behind every facade lies a unique narrative shaped by a myriad of experiences, dreams, fears, and triumphs.

By adhering to this principle, we embrace a mindset of openness and curiosity, recognizing that true understanding requires patience, empathy, and a willingness to explore beyond the surface. It prompts us to withhold judgment until we have taken the time to listen, observe, and empathize with others' perspectives.

Moreover, "Don't judge a book by its cover" challenges us to confront our own biases and preconceptions, urging us to question the validity of our initial impressions and to approach each encounter with humility and an open mind.

In embracing this lesson, we cultivate a culture of empathy, compassion, and inclusivity, fostering deeper connections and mutual respect among individuals from diverse backgrounds and walks of life. Ultimately, by looking beyond the superficial, we uncover the richness and depth of human experience, enriching our lives with a tapestry of stories and perspectives waiting to be explored.

My First Love

# CHAPTER 4: BRIAN

*The one who romanced me*

> *"Nothing is yours permanently so you better*
> *enjoy it while it's happening"*
> *-Joan Rivers*

M y teenage years were a whirlwind of rebellion, laughter, and unforgettable experiences. It all started when I first met Jill through a mutual friend who introduced us at a gathering. Jill was two years older than me, and I felt she was worldly. Jill had an innocent charm about her, yet I knew she was up for anything.

Jill was petite, with striking good looks. She had a twinkle in her eye that caught my attention. I understood that twinkle as meaning she was open to adventure and fun. I instinctively knew she would be my ride or die. Little did we know that this chance meeting would blossom into a lifelong friendship filled with roller skating escapades, late-night adventures, and endless mischief.

Roller skating was our favorite pastime. Mind you, this was the seventies, where bell bottoms, disco, and skates set you free. We made plans to meet up at the local rink, excited to glide across the polished floor in our rented skates. With combs in our back pocket and extra lip gloss in tow, we hit the rink with teenage abandon. I met my girlfriend Jill at the rink. I noticed that some cute guy was staring at me. You know that feeling you get when someone is staring at you? He asked me to skate and I left Jill in the dust to skate with my new cute boy.

Teenagers are fickle. Even stupid. Jill and I were the center of attention anywhere we went. We walked into a room, and people wanted to talk to us. We were magnets, which would prove to be a tool I used as I got older.

My mother always made sure I had a friend along when we went out, whether it was Diane or Jill. Our favorite spot to hang out became the Fountain Blue, where we spent countless hours laughing, gossiping, and sharing secrets. From our first visit to indulging in new foods to crashing legendary parties, we were always ready for an adventure.

With both our mothers preoccupied with their own lives, we found ourselves with plenty of freedom and little supervision. This lack of oversight allowed us to do pretty much whatever we wanted, often getting into mischief without consequence.

Diane and Jill, my ride or dies

Me and my rockstar Brian

We even seemed to tempt trouble when we were babysitting. Parents beware. Don't hire someone like me as your babysitter. While I love kids, at the time I would not be considered responsible. One memorable babysitting escapade ended with us getting into hot water after I threw Jill into a pool and we were caught sleeping at the house. And who could forget the time we hid guys in the shower when the mom came home early? Yep, I can't forget this. Teenage hijinks were a way of life. I wasn't made to be a babysitter, and that was a fact. I learned that my ability to push boundaries knew no bounds.

Our mischievous antics extended beyond babysitting gigs. On a lazy beach day at the shore, we lost the keys to my room at the Thunderbird hotel, and my mother made us dig in the sand at the beach until we found them, all because of a careless mistake. Then there were the days we cut school and sought refuge in the garage, hoping to avoid any unwanted attention. Imagine how much we got away with? And Mom was none the wiser.

Our circle of friends expanded over the years; however, Diane and Jill were my ride-or-dies. From clearing out places with DTs to waiting on street corners for hot guys to buy us beer, Jill's fearless attitude always kept us on our toes. Her bold way of navigating life excited me.

As we entered our early teens, experimenting with alcohol became a rite of passage. We started with Boone's Farm apple wine, shared with the Friedman twins, before eventually graduating to shots of rum and Southern Comfort.

Despite our rebellious streak, we still managed to take care of ourselves, cooking, doing laundry, and babysitting to earn a few extra bucks. But no matter how innocent our intentions, we always found ourselves in hot water, especially when we heard the garage door opening, signaling the imminent return of parental figures.

Our escapades reached a climax when we were asked to pack our bags and sent home early from a vacation, thanks to our unruly behavior. But even in the face of consequences, we remained unapologetically ourselves, always pushing boundaries and testing limits.

Through it all, our friendship remained steadfast, a bond forged in the fires of teenage rebellion and mischief. And though we may have caused our fair share of trouble, we wouldn't have traded those wild teenage years for anything in the world.

Mom would say, "Kimberlee, one day I hope you have a child that pays you back."

*Don't worry, Mom, I did.*

## THE FIRST BOY

My initiation into the world of love began in high school, amidst the anticipation of prom night. I looked like a movie star that night and was ready for the fairy tale prom elicits. A dashing boy, whisking me away in his father's Mercedes, set the stage for an unexpected encounter with my first love, Brian. Brian was not my prom date; in fact, he was at the prom with another girl. His cool demeanor and infectious personality left an indelible mark on me from the moment we met. A musician in a band, Brian's love for music was an aphrodisiac. His fingers gliding over the strings of the guitar, his mastery of the piano, drums, and vocals sent shivers down my spine.

As fate would have it, my friend inadvertently sparked Brian's interest by sharing tales of my reserved nature. Can you believe it? I was shy! Little did I know, Brian had taken a liking to me. When my prom date's deceit came to light, I swiftly severed ties, clearing the path for Brian to step in.

Immersing myself in the world of Brian's band, I found myself drawn to the lead singer's charm. A beach trip w

*However, Brian had his own plans.*

With precise execution, Brian and the singer's brothers orchestrated a serenade on the boardwalk, hoping to catch my attention. And catch it they did. Amidst the music, I found myself gravitating toward Brian, leaving behind the uncertainty of my previous relationship. Brian oozed romance. Everything he did was with poetic grace. I loved him, and he loved me.

The icing on the cake was Brian's family. Meeting his mother was a breath of fresh air. She greeted me with a glass of mint iced tea and a hug. I adored her style and the way she smudged kohl liner beneath her eyes. His parents loved each other and were kind and respectful to each other. It was a love I had never seen before, something I dreamed about since I was a little girl.

Brian's mom walked into a room, and her husband looked at her like it was the first time he saw her. I had never seen such love. Their family was a cohesive unit that brimmed with respect and admiration. Every time I was in their home, I was transported to a family life I dreamed of.

Dreaming of Being The Perfect Wife, Brian and Mrs. Drago

## THIS WAS MY DREAM!

Brian proved to be a devoted boyfriend, and eventually, he became my first love. He was gregarious, kind, and thoughtful — the kind of boy every mother wants her daughter to marry.

Though our physical intimacy took time to blossom, I made it clear to Brian that my heart was set on a future built on commitment and marriage. No sex before marriage, I told Brian. It was a reflection of my innocent dreams of being someone's beloved wife, a sentiment that now seems quaint in retrospect.

"Brian," I said with the innocence of an 18-year-old, "Are you going to marry me?"

Brian grabbed my waist and confirmed, "Of course I want to marry you, Kim. It is you and me always — together forever, I promise." His deep brown eyes seared into mine. I knew we were meant to be.

I said yes. He would be my "first." I felt at the time it would be forever. He began to unbutton my blouse, and while I was nervous, I knew I was ready.

Like teenagers do, we snuck a moment in Mom's house. I was so in love at the time I thought my heart was going to burst. Brian laid me down on Mom's pink shag rug and he kissed me. We gave into our teenage desires and I lost my virginity.

Right after the deed was done, we heard the garage door open. "BRIAN!" I screeched, "Oh my god, Mom is back!" I buttoned my blouse, and Brian straightened his ruffled hair and bounced up from the floor. You can't make this stuff up — it's as though Mom had a radar.

Any mother would have handpicked Brian to be her son-in-law. He was charming, came from a wonderful family, and was genuine. However, my mom felt I was too young to be in a serious relationship. Thus, this was the end of my first love affair.

Despite the twists and turns of love, the idyllic vision of candlelit dinners and waiting for a husband never materialized. Yet, in Brian's embrace, I found a love that felt genuine and enduring, shaping my understanding of romance and commitment for years to come. Although Brian and I were not meant to be, he set the bar high.

Me and Brian with my family

## JERSEY FLASHBACK

Flashback to my first reunion! I arrived at the hotel, and Caroline and some of the other cast members were in the lobby. Caroline tried to convince me to go easy on Joe Gorga, but I wasn't interested in her opinion. I was thrilled about the reunion though. Bravo had booked me a room at the Borgata, and I brought along my trusted confidante and friend, Kristen.

The next day, a producer came to my room and handed me a DVD with the last two episodes, including the Son Cubano drama. I was shocked to hear the names Joe Gorga was calling me when I wasn't there. I was seething.

When I went to Teresa's room for hair and makeup, Joe Giudice could tell I was furious and began filling my head with juicy gossip about Joe Gorga. I was locked and loaded.

The reunion filming dragged on, and since I was going to be the last guest, they allowed Kristen and me to go have dinner. Of course, I had a drink or possibly two! When they said it was time, I insisted Kristen come with me. The producer objected, but I stood my ground, and Kristen and I were off to the filming.

Kristen was incredibly nervous for me, but I remained as cool as a cucumber. Andy asked his first question, but I was interrupted by Joe Gorga, who pleaded to speak. I shut him down, but Andy requested to hear him out. Joe proceeded to apologize for the Son Cubano incident for a good 10 minutes. Even though I didn't want to accept his apology, Andy asked me to, and since he was my boss, I obliged.

Me and Kristen, My Surrogate Little Sister

Throughout the reunion, I was repeatedly asked if Teresa knew about Melissa being set up, and I staunchly defended Teresa, much to the producers' dismay. I genuinely believed Teresa didn't know what was going down. Only the producers knew exactly how they wanted to play that scene.

## MORAL OF THE STORY

You deserve romance- to be swept off your feet.

Never settle for anything less. The truth is that every person inherently deserves to be treated with respect, kindness, and love. This encompasses not only how others treat you but also the standards you set for yourself and the environments you choose to surround yourself with.

In romance, it's crucial to recognize your own value and refuse to settle for anything less than genuine love and mutual respect. This entails understanding your own needs, boundaries, and desires, and having the courage to communicate them effectively in relationships. It also means being willing to walk away from situations or individuals that do not meet your standards or contribute positively to your well-being.

Deserving the best extends beyond romantic relationships to encompass all aspects of your life. Whether it's your career, friendships, personal goals, or self-care practices, prioritizing your own happiness and fulfillment is essential for leading a fulfilling and meaningful life.

By internalizing the belief that you deserve the best, you empower yourself to make choices that align with your values and aspirations, and you cultivate a mindset of abundance and self-respect. This mindset not only attracts positive experiences and relationships into your life but also serves as a foundation for personal growth, resilience, and fulfillment.

In essence, embracing the fact that you deserve the best is an act of self-love and empowerment that sets the stage for a life filled with love, joy, and fulfillment in all its forms.

Me Getting Glammed Up

# CHAPTER 5: JOEY

*The one that got away*

> *"You'd think, 'What if I make a mistake today, I'll regret it'.
> I don't believe in regret, I feel everything leads us to where
> we are and we have to just jump forward, mean well,
> commit and just see what happens."*
>
> *- Angelina Jolie*

We all have that love that got away. We all have a regret that makes us think, "What IF"? I often ask myself, "What if I had made this choice, where would my life be right now?" I always answer to myself, I am exactly where I am supposed to be.

I had a lot of WHAT IF moments when I thought about Joey. Joey was the boy every mom dreams of marrying their daughter. Joey was the one who was gentle, respectful, and promised a white picket fence with two adorable kids.

Demes, Joey's father, was a gentleman who resembled Frank Sinatra and had been like an uncle to me. I had known him and his wife, Rocki, since before I could remember. This dynamic couple was a constant in my life. Rocki later became my sponsor for my confirmation. They were trusted, supportive, and offered me the tight family structure I craved.

Rocki and Demes formed a tight-knit husband and wife team, and their home became a second refuge for me alongside their two sons, Joey and Chucky. I bonded with their two sons and lapped up sun-filled afternoons in Miami by the pool whenever I had a chance.

At 15, Demes entrusted Joey, his oldest son, to my care.

"Joey," Demes said, "Joey, I want you to take Kim out for a nice time. Be her friend, be a gentleman." Joey accepted the challenge.

## OH THAT POOR BOY!

Joey was a tall, handsome, and intelligent young man destined for a medical career. In fact, Joey became a renowned cardiac surgeon in the New York area.

Joey, at 19, looked like he was out of a page of Esquire Magazine. His tanned physique always turned heads wherever we went. I felt safe with Joey and eager to experience Miami nightlife.

Our escapade led us to a club misleadingly named Swingers Lounge at the Newport Hotel in Miami. The Swingers Lounge was a hotspot more suited for young revelers like ourselves. There were no swingers involved. Ever.

This was an iconic club that I needed to be a part of. Can you imagine at 15, that I wanted to be a part of this nightlife scene? I felt like I was an adult and dressed myself in a pink mini skirt and white knee-high boots. My hair was long, blonde, and clipped with two barrettes. I felt invincible.

Despite my youthful appearance, Joey urged me to shed my childish barrettes to blend in. "Kimmy," Joey whispered as we were about to enter the club, "Kimmy, ditch those barrettes, it will make you look more mature."

I did not know barrettes would be a tip-off to my age. I trusted Joey and took the barrettes out. We walked up to the bouncer, and with no questions asked, we were escorted into the club.

Oh my, I can't believe it was this easy to get into a club," I thought. We were treated like VIPs. This was my first taste of an electric atmosphere, and an entryway into my love for opulence and high-energy nightclubs.

As we enjoyed the night with friends, I remained oblivious to Joey's unspoken affection, restrained by the three-year age gap between us. I would catch Joey smiling at me from afar, but that was all. Joey was a gentleman and would never take advantage of a young girl's innocence. He abstained from making any move.

Joey and Miami gave me a taste for adventure, and I was ready for the next one. I said goodbye to Joey, packed my bags, and headed to the Caribbean with my family and my bestie, Jill.

Curaçao is a diamond in the Caribbean. The salty winds were perfumed with the scent of the kibrahacha flower, which blanketed the island in its piercing yellow hue.

What's very special about this tree's bloom is that it requires long periods of drought before it has a chance to shine. It is normally a very drab-looking tree, but after a length of drought and the second rainfall, the trees will usually bloom into their wonderful yellow colors. I too felt my drought end and was ready to bloom.

Jill and I bloomed as we effortlessly navigated the casinos and clubs with the ease of someone beyond my years. I caught the club bug and was intoxicated by the nightlife.

By the time I turned 18, my visits to Miami became more frequent. In the opulent atmosphere of Coconut Grove, I reunited with Joey. Joey and I found ourselves drawn to each other with an intensity that could not be denied. Our connection grew into a sweet affair, and we made promises of a future together once he completed his studies. We were convinced that we were each other's perfect match, committed to our shared dreams.

Joey was the one for me. He was the perfect package. Nothing would come between our love for each other. He was every mother's ideal match for their daughter.

Joey, are we going to get married?" I asked. I felt my dream of becoming someone's wife was within reach. Joey was in medical school, and he proved to be solid husband material.

"Yes, Love," Joey would respond. Joey was solid, respectful, and smart—everything a girl would want. Yet, for some reason, this was not enough for me. I loved Joey, yet, I still needed more. More excitement. More adventure. More of everything.

Wanting more, feeling drawn to powerful, and often toxic influences seemed to be my future. While I adored Joey, it was easy to walk away. Perhaps it was my youth, naivety, or my insatiable need for excitement.

I craved excitement and was easily drawn to the illusion of power. My life and my love interests took an unexpected turn when I crossed paths with Frank, a charismatic wise-guy who ignited a different kind of passion within me. Without confronting my inner turmoil, I succumbed to self-sabotage, forsaking the stability and promise of Joey's love for the allure of riskier romance. I turned my back on a solid relationship and swapped it for danger, passion, and money. While I do not regret meeting Frank, and ultimately having our son Christopher, this decision led me down a dark path.

Looking back, I can't help but wonder how different my life might have been had I chosen to marry Joey. He became a respected heart surgeon. He was strong, respected, handsome, and saving lives. I question my flippant decision to leave Joey and jump into the dangerous bed of a mobster. Our decisions, however small they may seem in the moment, shape the trajectories of our lives in profound ways, steering us along paths we may never have imagined.

Me and Joey

## JERSEY FLASHBACK

Let's dive into another memorable flashback! I was invited with Kim G to Teresa's housewarming party, and we were both sipping on cosmos, feeling pretty good. The cameras were rolling, capturing every moment of the festivities. Teresa took the mic to thank her friends, which naturally included the cast. As I stood there, soaking in the atmosphere, something unexpected happened.

Out of nowhere, the producer Carlos King nudged me forward toward Teresa. Suddenly, it appeared to the audience that I was interrupting her speech! Caught off guard, I quickly composed myself and seized the moment. "Teresa," I said, "I love your house, and this is a fantastic party!" It was one of those behind-the-scenes moments orchestrated by the producers to add an extra twist to the storyline. Little did I know then how these small maneuvers behind the scenes would become integral to the drama that unfolded on screen.

## MORAL OF THE STORY

You are right where you are supposed to be.

In the journey of life, there are no rearview mirrors, no 'what ifs' that can alter the path already traveled. Every twist, turn, and detour has led you precisely to where you stand today. Embrace the notion that you are exactly where you are meant to be. Each experience, each decision, has sculpted your present reality. Look forward with unwavering confidence, for the future holds endless possibilities, awaiting your embrace. Trust in the journey, for it has guided you to this moment, and it will lead you to the brilliance that lies ahead.

The Perfect Wife- My First Wedding

# CHAPTER 6: FRANK

*The one I married.*

> *"Act as if you're a wealthy man, rich already, and you will become rich. Act as if you have unmatched confidence, and people will have confidence in you. Act as if you have all the answers, and the answers will come to you."*
> — *Jordan Belfort, Wolf of Wall Street*

It was at Gaspars, a pulsating super club, where I first crossed paths with the man who would become my first husband. Surrounded by his entourage (one of whom happened to be a cousin of mine), I locked eyes with Frank.

Frank exuded an aura of authority that intrigued me. I loved the energy of this masculine group; it felt powerful. Power is an aphrodisiac for me. A powerful man has the ability to walk through a crowd and demand anything he wants. He is confident and someone people respect.

Little did I know, Frank was deeply entrenched in a world I had yet to fully comprehend. Sounds familiar? I was repeating what I saw as a child, between Mom and Butchie.

Power. Allure. Luxury. These excited me. I was like a moth to a flame, much like how Mom felt when she met her second husband, Butchie. There's something about a bad boy that I was drawn to.

With an age gap of eleven years between us, he stood as a towering figure of influence, his connections tracing back to the powerful Genovese family. Knowing what I know now, a big gap in age suggests control. I was easy to control because I was young and in love with the dream of marriage.

In my youthful naivety, I was drawn to his extravagant lifestyle, reveling in the hedonistic pleasures of New York City's nightlife at the tender age of twenty-two. I craved being in Frank's circle. He opened doors for me that I could not imagine at such a young age.

He painted a picture of separation, living in a sprawling house where he claimed his only companions were his children. He told me his wife lived upstairs and he was relegated to the basement. He said he only stayed because of his kids. I was going to be a stepmom at an early age, and it did not faze me — or at least, this is what I told myself.

After all, Butchie, my stepfather, took me in as his own. Blinded by love and intoxicated by the allure of his world, I failed to see the warning signs that whispered of danger lurking beneath the surface. These signs looked like a person who needed control. He wanted to know every move I made, yet he disguised it as concern and love. He gave me what I needed at this time in my life, and I refused to see the dark underbelly of his life. That is what love can do. Love can blind you.

Our relationship was a whirlwind of excess, fueled by his boundless wealth and my insatiable appetite for adventure. He whisked me away to places where I didn't belong, exposing me to risks I was oblivious to, like a journey into the depths of Harlem to meet with ominous figures bearing suitcases and guns. I was all dolled up, and Frank was ready for a night on the town.

"Babe," Frank said, "I gotta make a stop."

I was compliant and trusting. "Ok, my love," I answered, as I applied lipstick in the visor mirror. We headed to the bowels of Harlem, and I felt the sting of anxiety. "Frankie, where we goin'?"

Frank got out of the car and was met with three dark figures. He shook their hands and hopped back in the car. As he tossed the briefcase in the back of the car, he smiled, "Baby, this is going to make us even richer!"

Despite the ominous undertones, I remained unfazed, my focus fixated solely on the next extravagant dining experience or lavish outing. Ignoring the doubts that lingered in the back of my mind, I surrendered to the superficial allure of his lifestyle, oblivious to the consequences that loomed on the horizon.

Me and Frank

My mother, wise to the dangers that surrounded me, confronted him one day, demanding answers to questions I had been too blinded to ask.

"Frank, what are you doing with such a young girl?" Mom questioned.

"Dorothy, Kim will do what she wants to do". Frank quipped with bravado. He knew what he wanted and was going to get it.

"Frank, you are messing with a young girl, you know your life is not safe-why would you do this to someone you care about?" Frank did not respond, but he knew he won the battle because I stuck by his side.

With unwavering resolve, she severed ties, presenting him with a choice that would alter the course of my life forever. "Kim-if you are going to remain with this man then you are out of my house" " Mom declared.

*I chose Frank.*

In a bold move that gave a nod to my youthful age, I moved in with Frank. I kissed mom goodbye and packed my bags. I embraced my newfound independence, leaving behind the comforts of mom's lavish lifestyle to forge a path of my own. Yet, even as I reclaimed my autonomy, I couldn't shake the realization of the materialistic tendencies that had clouded my judgment. It is true, I was drawn to money and power.

Reflecting on those tumultuous times, I recognize the recklessness of my actions, driven by a desire for wealth and status that obscured the humanity of those around me. It was a period defined by opulence and excess, where the trappings of luxury masked the darker truths lurking beneath the surface. And as I stepped away from that world, I vowed to chart a new course guided by authenticity and empathy, leaving behind the superficiality that had once defined me.

Being rich is intoxicating. Having anything you want at your fingertips can trump even the soundest of judgment, and this is what Frank offered me. Frank and I began a new chapter together, moving into a luxurious high-rise apartment overlooking the dazzling skyline of New York City. With my eye for design, I transformed our space into a chic oasis, adorned in shades of gray, black, and mirrors that reflected the sophistication of our urban lifestyle. I felt like my dream was coming true. I was committed to becoming a wife and doing it with panache.

However, amidst the luxury of being with Frank, doubts began to creep into my mind. I did not trust him. Frank would say one thing and do another. Frank was flashy and tried to dazzle me with a lifestyle steeped in fine dining, fashion, and wealth.

Seeking clarity, I fled to Florida, finding solace in the company of a dear friend in Sarasota. Little did I know, my friend's roommate happened to be none other than Cher's closest confidante, offering me unexpected counsel during a time of uncertainty. Yes, it is that Cher, the wife of Sonny. Despite their attempts to dissuade me from returning to Frank and his tumultuous world,

I ultimately succumbed to his allure once more. This game of ping pong proved to be exhausting. I relented and accepted his marriage proposal. After all, my dream was to become someone's wife.

Our union was sealed in a lavish wedding ceremony, my gown a masterpiece of handcrafted leather and lace, symbolizing the blend of luxury and edginess that defined our relationship. Frank whisked me away on a whirlwind European adventure, from the romantic streets of Rome to the sun-drenched cliffs of Positano, where our indulgent stay was unexpectedly footed by a shadowy gambling debt. I was whisked away by the romance of Italy, not knowing what would come next.

Leather and Lace

**What came next was a life changer.**

As the euphoria of our travels faded, reality set in with the news of my pregnancy. Positive. I was going to be a mother. I did not expect it to happen this quickly, but I was over the moon. I knew the hoopla was over. The flashy evenings out, drinking and galavanting had to end. Frank and I were going to be parents. We were man and wife. We were building a family. It was everything I dreamed of. Yet it was not. More often than not, we lie to ourselves. We lie to ourselves because it is comfortable and change is hard.

Me and My Christopher, Age Two

The doctor confirmed I was pregnant. I was scared and excited at the same time. I found comfort in bowl after bowl of pasta. I enjoyed watching my belly expand and feeling the flutters of life. *I can do this*, I thought. *I am ready to be a mother.* I had my handsome husband, albeit erratic, and a nice home.

A baby would complete this picture of domestic bliss. However, at the same time, I was nervous. Frank was becoming more unstable and his absence in the evenings frightened me.

With the onset of a new pregnancy I began to recognize that things were not right. I began to question Frank's activities.

*Why was Frank out galavanting? What was he doing? Who was he with?*

In retrospect, I was reliving the life I witnessed with Mom and Butchie. Mom was married to a mobster, and so was I. Mom did not ask too many questions, and I rarely questioned Frank. I knew intuitively that Frank was not the man I should be united with. Yet I told myself lies. I soothed my rattled nerves by telling myself, once the baby is born, Frank will come around and be the husband I needed.

Listen to me—never deviate from that gut feeling that is telling you something is wrong. You know the feeling, that little nudge in the back of your brain that tells you to run like hell? Don't ignore this.

**Run. Like. Hell.**

He was, at his core, a decent person, but he had dark edges that bled into our personal lives. These edges grew to take over my mind and induced anxiety. This anxiety grew to panic as I felt things were not right.

73

Yet, I lied to myself again. I held a strong feeling that the baby inside of me would bring us closer together, or so I thought. If you take one thing from my story, know that bringing a baby into a bad relationship will not solve your problems. In fact, a baby will make it worse.

Welcoming our son into the world should have been a joyous occasion, yet it marked the beginning of our downward spiral. Frank loved being a father and beamed with pride when he held Christopher. However, his bad behaviors continued to escalate.

While I embraced the responsibilities of motherhood, Frank continued to revel in his nocturnal escapades, leaving me isolated and disillusioned. Frank was a mobster, not a husband. The one person I have ever been able to count on, Dorothy, my mother, stood by my side and advised.

Mom knew one day I would see the truth in Frank, and she was ready to help me. She was a remarkable grandmother, doting on Christopher and helping me through postpartum. She sensed my intense unhappiness. The strain on our marriage became unbearable as Frank's partying became the center of his life. His friends lingered late into the night while I tended to our child alone. I would stay up late at night comforting our infant, hysterical because my husband was absent.

This is not how it's supposed to be," I thought. It became evident that our paths had diverged, and the love I once felt for him began to wane, overshadowed by a sense of outgrowing our tumultuous bond. He found himself in unsavory deals and partnerships. I did not want this for myself or our son. Christopher was everything to me. I looked into his eyes and knew that this is not the life I wanted to give my son. While I loved the idea of Frank, I did not feel safe with him.

Frank's desperation turned to violence when I broached the subject of divorce, his threats chilling me to the core. In a frightening moment of brutality, he unleashed his fury upon me, leaving scars both physical and emotional. With sheer determination, I fled our home, taking refuge with my family as I navigated the aftermath of our shattered marriage, with my baby in tow.

The ensuing years were fraught with danger as Frank's obsession with control spiraled. Yet, amidst the chaos, my stepfather's intervention provided a glimmer of hope, his plea to Frank's superiors a last resort to safeguard my life. Butchie was still my protector, but his insertion into our domestic hell had little effect on Frank. In the face of such darkness, it was the support of loved ones that guided me through the storm, reminding me of the resilience of the human spirit in the face of adversity.

In a situation where fear and shock would be the natural response, I found myself once again defying the norm, propelled forward by an unwavering determination to reclaim my life. Let's get this clear, I am not afraid of telling the truth, but I was scared of my husband's violent reaction. Frank was capable of a lot of things and I did not want to be another statistic.

> *According to the U.S. Department of Justice, domestic violence is characterized as a recurring pattern of abusive actions within any relationship. These actions are employed by one partner with the intention of gaining or maintaining control over the other intimate partner.*
>
> - **Domestic Violence Statistics in the United States in 2024 - EarthWeb**

I knew that if I left, it meant his family left. I had to be smart. I summoned the courage to pack my bags and leave Frank. I did not focus on his retaliation; I just needed to get out. By all accounts, I was a relentless force of nature, undeterred by the shadows that lurked in his wake. I knew I had to make a move. I was desperate. Frank was knee-deep in illegal transactions. He was barely able to connect with his wife and child. And the violence was escalating. If I did not do something, I would be led down the path of misery.

**THE SUMMER AWAY**

Taking immediate action, my mother and I withdrew the funds from the bank where we deposited all the checks we received as wedding gifts. I sought refuge down the shore, where the ocean breeze whispered promises of freedom. I am a Jersey Girl through and through, and I am drawn to the salty air of the shore. The shore is always a place of peace for me, and I knew it would be a healthy space for Christopher and me to bond. Securing a spacious townhouse near the beach, I called my closest friends to join me in this sanctuary of solace and renewal. I needed my girls to surround and support me.

My gal pals obliged, packed their bags, and joined me at the shore. We had girl time, long afternoons on the beach, and fun-filled evenings. This escape was what I needed at the time. It restored my soul. Yet, Frank was always near, unraveling this quiet space with threats and anger. He combed the streets, interrogated my family and friends, and made it known that no woman of his would disrespect him.

Amidst the chaos, I found an unexpected ally in the form of a young woman on the cusp of embracing a life of devotion. I needed help with Christopher, and Rita needed a reason to break free from her current path.

Rita came into my life right when I needed her. She was on the cusp of devoting herself to God and becoming a nun. Can you imagine a young woman ready to join the cloisters of a nunnery, choosing to live her life alongside me?

We both saved each other. She saved me by supporting me as a single mother, and I saved her by allowing her to live a life of freedom.

Arriving straight from the convent to serve as my nanny, she grappled with the abrupt shift from the seclusion of her religion to the vibrant pulse of our beachside retreat. Yet, despite her initial reluctance, she soon found her footing, which was a testament to her strength in the face of newfound freedom.

Rita, my nanny and Christopher

Buoyed by the spirit of liberation, I immersed myself in the heady euphoria of summer, seizing every opportunity to experience a slice of my independence. From wild nights out on the town to the exhilarating rush of romance, each moment became proof of the resilience of the human spirit. I felt alive again.

For a moment, Frank's proverbial handcuffs were unlocked, and it felt good. His need to control me was palpable even when I thought I was free. It was amidst this liberation that I met a charming native who drew me in with his charm. He was a steelworker by day and a bartender by night. His sculpted physique and magnetic smile drew me in like a moth to a flame. *Damn, he was hot.* This is exactly what I needed at the time.

This Adonis swept me off my feet and ignited passion into my soul. I yearned for our secret rendezvous. Sometimes, a distraction like this can help you heal. However, in reality, it was just a temporary band-aid. As our connection deepened, reality intruded, reminding me that the bliss of summer must eventually yield to the harsh light of day. A brief love affair was not the answer to my marital problems.

**Back To Reality**

Returning to the confines of my mother's house marked the resurgence of old threats and renewed fear, as Frank's relentless pursuit cast a shadow over our separation. His presence loomed ominously, a constant reminder that the specter of danger was never far behind.

With each passing day, the stakes grew higher, as Frank's desperation manifested in chilling displays of aggression.

Armed with a gun and fueled by vengeance, he prowled the streets in search of me, leaving a trail of fear and uncertainty in his wake. It would frighten even the strongest of people. Frank was on a mission to destroy me.

Frank was angry. His eyes were dark, and his hands were ready to strike. In one moment of rage, Frank grabbed me and wrapped his fingers around my neck. The venom of his vengeance spewed as his teeth clenched around my nose. The father of my child, the man I married, left his teeth marks on my face. This permanent scar on my face was a reminder of his uncontrollable rage.

**Never, ever let anyone put hands on you. EVER!**

At this moment, I grabbed what mattered: my son, and left everything else behind. I ran as fast as I could. I never looked back. However, Frank was a predator. He would not let go of what he believed was his. I recognized that I was Frank's possession. Christopher was Frank's possession. Frank did not like to lose what he believed he owned. Yet, even in the face of such darkness, I refused to cower in the shadows, drawing strength from the bonds of friendship and the resilience of the human spirit. Forged in the crucible of adversity, my resolve remained unbroken. I still had hope amidst this storm. I declared my independence from the shackles of a toxic marriage.

**Yet, I needed help.**

I pulled in the force of my family. My second step-father, Tommy Granatell, took over. He knew I needed help and Frank needed to learn a lesson. Tommy had a sit down with Frank and his "bosses".

Tommy knew that he needed to have a man-to-man conversation with my husband and the violent threats needed to end now. "Frank", Tommy warned, "You need to leave Kim alone. Let her raise your son in peace". Frank, the archetype of an alpha-male, looked Tommy in his eyes and pushed back, "Tom, I can do whatever I want when it comes to Kim and our kid. They are mine".

My Handsome Son, Age 7

Frank sat back in his chair and began tapping his fingers on the table to add credence to his position. Frank always wanted to have the upper hand. Frank's posture was stiff and commanding. However, Tommy did not back down. Tommy went into this meeting with one result in mind, and he knew he had an ally in the "bosses". Frank's "bosses" intervened in a not-so-diplomatic fashion and shut Frank down. "Frank", they said, "You will let Kim go. If you do anything to that girl, we will do something to you."

The message was received, and Frank backed down. While there were custodial issues that remained ever-present, Frank never touched me again. The rest is history.

## JERSEY FLASHBACK

As my car made its way to the filming location at Portabello restaurant, my mind buzzed with anticipation. With me were my mother and Kristen, the atmosphere filled with excitement and nerves. Suddenly, the calm of the car was pierced by the ringing of my phone, the sound echoing through the Bluetooth connection.

It was my head producer on the line, his voice carrying a sense of urgency. "Don't worry," he reassured me, "we have amped up security for tonight!" His words sent a jolt of surprise through me, and I couldn't help but exclaim, "WHAT?" My mother and Kristen, sitting beside me, mirrored my astonishment, their expressions a mix of disbelief and concern.

The producer's cryptic message left me bewildered. Did they really expect me to engage in a physical altercation with Joe Gorga? The rumor mill had been churning with speculation, particularly about Mel's alleged infidelity with her old boyfriend, Bulldog. With the filming set to involve the Gorgas, Wakiles, and Lauritas, tensions were running high.

As I entered the restaurant, the atmosphere crackled with anticipation. I was called over by the crew, and once again, I found myself defying the producers' expectations. Despite their hopes for drama, what they wanted did not come to pass.

Instead, we all reconciled, making amends over drinks. The evening took an unexpected turn, leaving the producers fuming as they departed. Later, MG pulled my mother aside, seeking to reassure her about her intentions. My mother, though cautious, found MG's sincerity convincing.

After the night's events, I found myself reflecting on the conversation I had with T, her denial ringing in my ears. Despite the chaos of the evening, one thing was clear: I was determined to navigate the murky waters of reality television on my own terms.

## MORAL OF THE STORY

**Love should not be scary. You are worth more.**

In the depths of youth, I found myself ensnared by the seductive allure of power. Like many, I believed it to be the ultimate measure of worth, the gold standard of validation in a world fraught with uncertainty. Yet, my journey down this dangerous path revealed a stark truth: the pursuit of external accolades and societal status is a treacherous illusion.

Through the haze of misguided ambition, I stumbled upon a revelation that shook me to my core. My worth, I realized, was not tethered to the trappings of success, but rather to the immutable essence of my being. In moments of solitary reflection, I unearthed the profound truth that my value lay in the unique qualities and strengths that defined me as an individual.

Armed with this newfound awareness, I embarked on a journey of self-discovery and empowerment. No longer shackled by the illusion of external validation, I found the courage to assert my boundaries and demand respect in the face of mistreatment. With each step forward, I reclaimed my dignity and forged a path guided by my own inner compass.

Reflecting upon my tumultuous journey, I am compelled to share this cautionary tale with others. For I have learned, through trial and tribulation, that the pursuit of power and validation outside oneself is a perilous endeavor. Let my story serve as a reminder that true empowerment and self-worth can only be found within, and that the siren song of external validation leads only to disillusionment and despair.

*You are worth more. Period.*

# CHAPTER 7: GEORGE

*The One Who Saved Me*

*"Storms Make Trees Grow Deeper Roots"*
*—Dolly Parton*

In the midst of a nasty divorce, you need to keep your friends close.

I spent five years trying to finalize a divorce that incited terror in my heart. Frank was angry. He wanted to see me suffer with every fiber of his being. Frank wanted revenge. His weapon of choice was Christopher.

Frank would go to the ends of the earth to punish me, and the visitation battle became one of epic proportions. I always maintained full custody of our son, and he always had me in court as he fought for visitation. Our frequent battles in court made me a regular. I quickly received the nickname "Ice Princess" due to my stoic nature. Oh boy, I loved this nickname!

Our uncoupling was nasty. When I say nasty, I mean threats, accusations, and manipulation. Frank knew my son was the most important thing to me, and he wanted to make me pay for our separation. At this time, Frank's drinking escalated. For all intents and purposes, his home was unsafe for Christopher. Frank still felt he was in control of me and attempted to manipulate the court proceedings. He demanded more visitation with his son. The thought of my innocent child spending time in Frank's toxic home rattled me to the core.

I get it. It is very important for a child to have love from both parents. I understood this. However, I also knew that my infant would be subjected to an unhealthy lifestyle as soon as he was under Frank's control. I had a fight on my hands and knew it was going to be an uphill battle. I was ready to go toe to toe with him.

Frank won visitation rights, and it scared the hell out of me. The wise judge (I am saying this with sarcasm) granted visitation and qualified this right by saying, "Kim, you allow your son to spend time with his father unless he is tripping over drunk. Otherwise, it is ordered that Frank has visitation rights." When the judge hit his gavel, the sharp crack echoed through the courtroom, sending shivers up my spine.

What judge in his right mind would allow an infant to spend time with a careless parent who lived a wild lifestyle? My judge did. This was a horrible miscarriage of justice. However, with time, I knew that the court would recognize Frank's toxic parenting style. Eventually, the court system would find my ex-husband guilty of breaking the law. His destructive patterns and illegal activities left him in prison for several years.

Frank was still pissed. Let me be clear, Frank was always pissed. He could not let go of his "imagined" family and wanted to make me suffer for destroying his family unit. This was more an issue of him trying to control everything around him. Control is an illusion. All we can control is what we think and how we behave.

At this time, Frank was focused on torturing me through our child. He would yell and scream at me. His rants were all Christopher-centered. Every time I would drop Chris off at his father's home, the chill of his hatred was evident.

One time, when I dropped our son off for visitation, I felt the numbness of anxiety creep through my body. I walked into Frank's foyer and handed Frank the diaper bag. "Christopher's snacks are in there, his diapers, and I put a change of clothes as well. I will be back at 5 pm".

Frank nodded and scooped up our son. Christopher giggled and gave his daddy a big kiss. Don't get me wrong, Christopher was always happy to see his father. Frank's house was always fun. There was always a flurry of activity, and there always was something good cooking on the stove.

I backed away from Frank and gave Christopher a big kiss goodbye. "Mommy loves you, Christopher". Leaving your child in a custody arrangement is always hard. You give up a bit of control of your child's experience. I simply had to trust the fact that Frank loved his son and would take good care of him.

As I walked down the driveway and opened my car door, I heard my name.

"Kim- KIM!", Frank hollered.

Oh my god, what is going on, I thought. My immediate thought was that something was going on with our son. I was always in fight-or-flight mode when I was around my ex-husband. The adrenaline was always pumping.

I looked up from my car door and saw Frank running out with a big smile on his face. "Kimmy- you gotta taste this meatball. Oh my god, this is the best, come on- taste it"!

Frank, the man who tortured me for so many years, passed along a peace offering. He held a fork with a big meatball dripping with gravy. He carried it over to me and smiled. "Come on Kimmy, it is to die for."

I took a nibble and smiled. "Frank, ya did good".

I jumped in my car and felt a little peace in my heart for the first time in ages. I saw a glimpse of the man I once loved. This brief interaction gave me joy.

**I knew Chris would be okay. I would be okay.**

This is when George entered the picture.

My Second Attempt At Being The Perfect Wife With George

George was large in stature, and his looks gave a nod to the handsome movie star Michael Douglas. George was dashing, adventurous, and strong. He was the man I thought would be my protector and put Frank in his place. I finally felt safe. I finally felt that Christopher had a chance at a normal upbringing.

George was my knight in shining armor. He swept me off my feet and lived a life of incredible highs and, sometimes, unending lows. Despite the friction in the relationship with Frank, George had my back.

So I married him. Yep, that's right. Husband number two came into my life this quickly. George got on his knee and offered me the promise of a beautiful life together.

And true to Kim D. style, it was an over-the-top affair at Le Cirque.

Le Cirque is iconic in New York. It is a mecca where food, fashion, and art collide. Throughout its various incarnations and relocations, Le Cirque has retained its unmistakable charm and allure. The restaurant's décor may have evolved, but its commitment to delivering an unforgettable dining experience remains unwavering. From the whimsical motifs of monkeys and circus balls to the elegant ambiance created by tent shades, Le Cirque continues to captivate diners with its unique blend of sophistication and playfulness.

*Can you imagine a wedding at such an establishment?*

Do not imagine any further, as it was the perfect epitaph for a wedding that was doomed from day one. While our public outings were filled with joy, our private life was marked by frequent arguments and isolation. Ultimately, I made the difficult decision to end the relationship for the sake of my well-being and my son's. Reflecting on our time together, I believe George rescued me from Frank's torment, offering protection and support throughout our tumultuous journey.

I loved George for saving me, yet, in retrospect, he was a place for me to escape the horrors of my first marriage. Let me tell you something, it takes two people to make a relationship work, and I don't believe either of us had the tools to be successful in this marriage.

I never gave up on my childhood dream of domestic bliss. I still wanted to be a wife and create a home and life that was beautiful.

I kept gravitating to this fantasy of being the perfect wife. I know now I was trying to force my second husband to be someone he was not. I still held on to the fantasy of being a perfect wife. I wanted to create a sacred space, care for my son, and enjoy out-of-the-box adventures with my spouse.

George didn't understand the reality of being married to me. He was fighting his own demons, and I will leave it at that. I can be a lot. I know you are thinking right now that this fact cannot be true. However, I can be a handful. Yes, doll, I am extra.

We were incompatible, but I so desperately wanted to create stability after coming out of an abusive relationship. I was not healed. Period.

George was kind to Christopher, which was the most important thing. However, as a married couple, we were disconnected. It did not work. I failed. I was never healed from my relationship with Frank.

When you face failure, you need to get real with yourself. I have failed many times, but I have reconciled the loss as a learning experience. Many of my friends have experienced failures like this, and I have little tolerance for self-pity.

Self-pity mires us in a cycle of bad habits. It is a friend like me who will say, "You have a few days to feel bad about yourself, then you get your ass up and learn the lesson you are supposed to learn."

George was my last and final husband. In a way, I gave up my dream of being a perfect wife. I started to understand that there was more to me than being a wife. I did not need a legal document to define me as a human being. After all, I was pretty damn strong. I am a single mother, a businesswoman, and I won't put up with bullshit any longer.

**I am Kim D. Hear me roar.**

## JERSEY FLASHBACK

Ah, the year when Melissa and Joe Gorga made their grand entrance onto the show! I remember it like it was yesterday. I was away with Michael when the call came through for Melissa to make her debut at Posche. Picture this: Melissa struts into Posche, oozing confidence, and declares, "Hi, I am Melissa Gorga, the new, younger, hot housewife." I was taken aback by her sheer audacity. Never before had I encountered someone so self-assured.

The night before the infamous Christening, I was on the phone with Teresa. She was torn about signing the contract, adamant that she didn't want to film with her family. My advice was simple: don't let them push you off a show that you started. It's good money, just go for it. And boy, did she ever. The next day, she showed up to film, and what ensued was nothing short of brutal. Joe Gorga unleashed his fury, acting like an animal, hurling insults at Teresa, banging on the table, and turning his son's christening into a chaotic mess.

But behind the scenes, away from the cameras, there was a moment of raw emotion that never made it to the screen. When Joe Gorga broke down, screaming at his father, "You are MY FATHER!" Mr. Gorga's response was swift and shocking—he smacked him across the face for his disrespectful behavior towards his sister.

Amidst all the chaos, I had my biggest fashion show that year. The Brownstone was packed to the brim, oversold by over 100 people. It was standing room only, with chairs crammed together, and every Real Housewife in attendance. Melissa Gorga, Teresa, and Jacqueline all strutted down my runway, while Caroline and Kathy watched from the audience. And let's just say, where there are Housewives, drama is never far behind!

## MORAL OF THE STORY

Heal yourself before you try to heal others.
Sometimes you win, sometimes you learn.

Life is a journey filled with victories and defeats, each offering its own unique opportunity for growth and self-discovery. Embrace both the highs and lows, for they shape who you are and pave the way for your future successes. Approach every experience with an open mind and a willingness to learn, and you'll find that even in moments of setback, there is wisdom to be gained. As you turn the page to the next chapter of your life, carry with you the understanding that every outcome, whether triumphant or challenging, contributes to your ongoing journey of becoming the best version of yourself.

Before you can fully extend a helping hand to others, it's essential to tend to your own well-being. Just as a healer must tend to their own wounds before aiding others, so too must you prioritize self-care and self-compassion. Take the time to heal your own hurts, nurture your spirit, and cultivate resilience within yourself. Only then can you offer genuine support and empathy to those around you. Remember, true strength lies not only in the ability to uplift others but also in the courage to acknowledge and address your own vulnerabilities. As you embark on the journey of healing, remember to tend to your own needs with the same kindness and dedication you extend to others.

Me and Jimmy

# CHAPTER 8: JIMMY

*The One Who Electrified Me*

> *"And I swear, you're just like a pill*
> *Instead of making me better*
> *You keep making me ill*
> *You keep making me ill"*
> *-P!nk, Just Like a Pill*

Jimmy was magnetic. Period. He walked into a room, and everyone wanted to be around him. Everyone who knew Jimmy wanted to be closer to him. Jimmy had a charisma no one could ignore. I became addicted to Jimmy.

His presence exuded charm, and being around him was like being swept up in a whirlwind of excitement and allure. I was drawn to his flashy demeanor, his romantic gestures, and the undeniable chemistry that crackled between us. Romance is everything to me, and Jimmy provided it.

After parting ways with George, I found myself navigating the single life once more. At that time, I was petite, almost tiny, with a daring short platinum bob framing my face. During one of our nights out, fueled by the promise of adventure and mingling, I met a girlfriend who shared my single status. Together, we found ourselves amidst a sea of flirtatious encounters, including a chance meeting with her recently estranged husband, whom we unwittingly helped reconcile.

When the couple got back together, they decided it was time to introduce me to his brother.

And then he walked in — Jimmy. With his striking good looks and undeniable presence, he captured my attention effortlessly. I loved everything about him: the way he walked, the way he smelled, the way he tasted. Late-night conversations and stolen kisses ensued, leaving me hungover and breathless the next day. Every day, I eagerly anticipated his call. I needed this man, and I needed to be close to him.

Every moment I was with him, I felt so high. Jimmy was my drug, and I needed more.

Jimmy, the esteemed restaurateur of JD's, wasted no time in sweeping me off my feet. A lunch date in Soho led to a whirlwind of restaurant-hopping, his demeanor belying any hint of marital obligations. His plans extended far beyond casual lunches, as he mentioned whisking me away to Europe, starting with Rome.

One thing you should know is that travel intoxicated me. The planning, the preparation, and the thrill of exploring exotic locations pulled me in like nothing else. When Jimmy said "vacation," I replied, "WHEN?"

Jimmy surprised me with tickets to Venice. "Kimmy, get ready for the cruise of a lifetime!"

In the romantic backdrop of a Venetian ship, our passion ignited, culminating in him gifting me a chandelier as a token of his affection. Jimmy was clear about what he wanted. He wanted to sail on Italian waters with his girl at his side. He orchestrated every moment of the high seas adventure. When we opened the door to our cabin, the look on Jimmy's face was priceless.

As he inspected our cabin, he immediately picked up the phone. "Yes, we are in cabin 523, and unfortunately, it needs attention now," Jimmy ordered. I loved his commanding manner.

"Yes, sir," the woman replied. "Sir, what is wrong?"

Jimmy responded, "There are two double beds here. There is no way in hell I am spending two weeks with my girl in two double beds. I need you to fix this immediately." Jimmy smirked at me, and true to his nature, he would remedy this issue. Within minutes, a purser knocked at the door and began to unscrew the two double beds to make them one.

Jimmy was this kind of guy. It was clear he was smitten, but beneath the surface lurked the shadows of his struggles with a darker side. His unwavering devotion to his children was admirable; however, I was often relegated to an afterthought.

From my vantage point, I would see Jimmy deep in thought, in which I could not penetrate. "Jimmy, what's wrong?" I asked. He would nod and motion me away. I could not compete with the demons in his head. I would often make excuses for his disinterest in me, but small feelings of doubt would bubble to the surface.

Back on home soil, the facade of passion began to crack under the weight of reality. Despite my efforts to dazzle him with my appearance and affection, I found myself relegated to the sidelines as Jimmy's attention remained steadfastly focused on his children.

I get it—children should be your first priority. My son Christopher is my everything. However, if you are building a life with a partner, it is important to bring them into your circle. It is important to facilitate positive relationships with the children of your partner.

Jimmy made it easy for me to be a surrogate caretaker for his kids. They were playmates for Christopher, and we had high adventures. I took them to ice cream shops, bowling, miniature golfing, and more. I always had an ample supply of their favorite cookies, ice cream, and toilet paper in the house. Yes, I said toilet paper. Charmin was the brand of choice for Jimmy and his family.

However, when Jimmy was around, I was invisible.

Everything I did was to get Jimmy's attention. I wanted to be the one woman he could not live without. Yet, his attention was scattered, leaving me with a sense of worthlessness. Jimmy was not an abusive man. In fact, he was the opposite. I witnessed internal battles that I did not understand at the time. All I wanted was to have a healthy relationship with this person, but he did not have the tools to meet me halfway.

Frustrated and disillusioned, I made the difficult decision to end things, refusing to settle for a relationship where I felt sidelined and unfulfilled. Yet, despite our breakup, the magnetic pull between us proved irresistible, drawing us back into each other's orbits time and time again. We could not stay away from each other because the chemistry was undeniable.

*I did not make a move until the universe gave me a wake up call.*

The phone rang.

It was Frank, my ex-husband.

"Kim," Frank began. His voice was faint and weak. This was not like Frank. Frank was strong, commanding, and often an asshole. "Kimmy, I am dying—I have cancer."

I was silent.

I remember these words like it was yesterday. I fell to the floor and just listened. I listened like no other day in my life.

"Kim, it is not good. It is terminal. They say it is my pancreas— and stage 4."

This man, who made me suffer for so many years, who gave me my beautiful son, who gave me a glimpse into a powerful and often a corrupt world, was dying. Frank was weak, remorseful, and I felt sorry for him.

"Frank," I began quietly, "I am here for you." A flood of emotions pulsed through me. Do you know the feeling? The feeling when you are there but you are not? It was an out-of-body experience.

Frank, my first husband, the man who was going to make my childhood dreams a reality, had only a few moments left on this earth. All I could do was feel sincere empathy for him. He made a lot of mistakes, yet, he was repentant.

"I am sorry, Kimberlee, for everything. You are a good mom. You are a fighter. No matter what, take care of Christopher. You are all he's got." This punch in the gut hit me hard.

The room started swirling as memories flooded into my consciousness. My mind became a Rolodex of memories. I began reminiscing about the good times, like the day we were married, the day Chris was born, the extravagant trips, and the over-the-top holidays. I chose to remember a kinder Frank at this moment. As I hung up the phone, I thought it was the last time I would ever hear his voice.

**Thirty days later Frank was dead.**

My anxiety hit a new high. *How was I going to tell Christopher? How was I going to cope with this man leaving earth?*

'Kim,' I thought, 'get your ass up and be the woman you know you are. You are strong,' I told myself. Yet, I did not have the energy to combat the demons of anxiety. I had a son, and I had to figure out how to be a mom during the darkest of times.

Every day, I struggled to get through the day after the passing of my son's father, which plunged me into a maelstrom of grief and uncertainty. When Frank died, a part of my history passed away. When our son Christopher heard the news, his little life changed forever. Chris was eleven and tried to be strong for me. No child should have the burden of 'being strong' after losing a parent. I could not bear to see my child in so much pain. In the midst of my turmoil, a dear friend's battle with pancreatic cancer served as a stark reminder of life's fragility. We all need reminders like this. The universe continues to provide us with the direction we are meant to be on.

I was being bombarded with life-altering events watching my son's deep grief, and I did not know how to be a good mother for him at this time. I knew I needed help.

**Let me tell you something, it is ok to ask for help.**

As a matter of fact, asking for help is a sign of strength. I went to my doctor with a sense of desperation and shared with him my story. I was pale, thin, and my mind was my enemy.

"Doc, I don't know what to do. I am so lost," I said.

"Kimberlee," his voice was calming, and I knew he would have an answer, "Kim, life gets hard and it is okay — sometimes we need to use medications to rewire our brains and give us the boost we need to get back on track."

Doc immediately wrote a prescription for Paxil. Paxil is a prescription medication for panic disorders.

*Oh how I know panic!*

Paxil works to balance a person's level of serotonin by preventing brain cells from quickly absorbing it. Through balancing serotonin levels, Paxil can help enhance mood and reduce anxiety. Millions of Americans who take antidepressants and similar medications are supported through their emotional journey by pharmaceutical intervention. However, many meds like Paxil do more than alleviate sadness. They may also dial down feelings of happiness and joy.

This flattening of feelings, called "emotional blunting," can leave you feeling numb to the world. I felt my emotions flatlining. And Jimmy was the receiver of this inability to feel. I could see, with clarity, Jimmy did not prioritize me in my life.

As I grappled with my emotions on Paxil, I came to the sobering realization that my relationship with Jimmy had left me feeling hollow and unfulfilled. My addiction to this man wavered. I could no longer make excuses for our broken relationship.

With a heavy heart, I returned the engagement ring and chose to walk away, determined to reclaim my sense of self-worth and strength. My decision to leave Jimmy was not because of Paxil; I simply realized that the fire had been extinguished. Paxil gave me the clarity to realize that I deserve more.

Embracing my newfound independence, I embarked on a journey of self-discovery, determined to rebuild the resilience that Jimmy's presence had eroded. Though the road ahead was uncertain, I knew that better days awaited me, free from the tumultuous highs and lows of our rocky relationship.

Reach out, speak up, and allow yourself the support you deserve. You are not alone, and there is strength in seeking the assistance you need to navigate life's challenges.

I asked for help, and it led to difficult yet healthy decisions. I left someone I was deeply in love with. If I had not left him, I would not have landed the role on Real Housewives. I would not have opened Posche. I would not have met the love of my life, Michael. AND, I would not have written this book. This independence led me to the gym. For all intents and purposes, I became a gym rat. I found a high in physical fitness. And damn, I looked good. Doing good things for ourselves leads us on new paths, and my path led me to the love of my life.

## JERSEY FLASHBACK

Fast forward to my first reunion. The nerves were palpable as we checked in and caught sight of the Manzos. Caroline pulled me aside, pleading, "Can you please take it easy on Joe G? Tell the truth, Kim." Little did I know, those DVDs they handed me would reveal the shocking truth of what transpired outside Son

Cubano. A year later, I was armed with knowledge, ready to take Gorga to task!

Clad in a purple satin Dolce and Gabbana number and gold 6-inch high Giuseppe Zanotti shoes, I was ready to rock. But running late, the producers whisked Kristen and me off for dinner at Bobby Flay Steaks at the Borgata Hotel. When it was time to hit the stage, they tried to separate us, but I put my foot down. Kristen was coming with me, no ifs, ands, or buts. And sure enough, she stood by my side.

Walking onto that stage, Kristen was a bundle of nerves, but I? Cool as a cucumber. Gorga tried to interject, but I shut him down. Andy asked if I'd accept his apology, and while it threw off my planned speech, I kept my composure. Then came the onslaught of questions about Strippergate. I had Teresa's back, much to the chagrin of the others. By the end of it, the tension was thick enough to cut with a knife, but it was one hell of an experience!

## MORAL OF THE STORY

**It is okay to ask for help.**

Life is short. Know what you want, who you are, and stop making excuses. Listen to the universe and stop ignoring the signs. When we resist what the universe is telling us, life gets really hard. It gets exhausting fighting for things that do not serve us.

And, it is okay to ask for help in our dark hours. Doll, if I did not seek support, I would not be here today. In a world that often glorifies self-sufficiency and independence, it's important to remember that it's perfectly okay to ask for help. Seeking out professionals who can guide you through your toughest moments isn't a sign of weakness; it's a courageous step towards healing and growth. None of us are immune to vulnerability, and pretending otherwise only adds unnecessary weight to our shoulders. Remember, it's okay to not be okay all the time.

Me and My Michael

# CHAPTER 9: MICHAEL

*The One Who Was The One*

> *"Love is a promise; love is a souvenir, once given,*
> *never forgotten, never let it disappear."*
> *— John Lennon*

My separation from Jimmy was tough. He was a magnet, and every day I fought to release myself from his pull. Breaking free from any relationship is difficult, and I knew I needed to do things differently. So I plunged, feet first, into working on myself.

I chose me.

This was the first time, ever, that I did not have a man at my side. To tell you the truth, it was freeing. There is freedom in focusing on what really matters. I saw it as my opportunity to get to know who Kim D. is without a man. I had to relinquish the desire to be a wife. In some ways, especially in the beginning, I felt like the little girl whose dream had faded. Yet, I felt a sense of pride the more I got to know this version of myself. This may sound corny, but I began dating myself.

Every day, I went to the gym. Let me tell you, the release of endorphins after a little time on the treadmill is the medicine that soothed my anxious mind. Every morning I would lace up my sneakers, put on a cute pair of yoga pants and a tank, then head over to Cando Fitness. Kenny, my shaved-head personal trainer, greeted me with a smile and then proceeded to kick my ass.

Me Choosing Me

I did squats, I did push-ups, I curled weights. I began to see a difference in my mood and my body. I was loving the single life. For years, I was a serial monogamist. I jumped from one husband to another or from one boyfriend to another boyfriend. You catch my drift. I was tired, and I wanted to improve myself before I gave my heart and soul away.

There is a sense of empowerment when you navigate your life on your own terms. I have to admit, there always was a faint whisper of forlorn at dinnertime when I did not have a partner to share my day with. But I got over this pretty quickly.

My confidence skyrocketed. I took care of Christopher during the days, packing his school lunches and dropping him off at the bus stop. My clothing business was bustling, my girlfriends were always there to support me, and my dogs were nipping at my toes. It was pure heaven.

I soaked up every moment. I was not tethered to another person's schedule, wants, or needs. If I wanted to do laundry on Mondays, I did. If I wanted to go out to dinner on a Wednesday, sure as hell I did. If I wanted to take Chris out for ice cream before dinner, you better believe that I did this. The world was my oyster.

It was almost one year of self-exploration that ignited a spark in me. Jimmy and I separated, I felt sad, and I reinvented myself. A pity-party was not an invitation I accepted.

I am, and always will be, a creature of habit, so change is always hard for me. I love myself a good, hearty Italian meal and found myself nestled at a local eatery once a week called Lunellos. This is the kind of restaurant that feels like home, that serves up the best chicken parm and arrabbiata sauce. When mom was watching Christopher, I always took the opportunity to call up my closest girlfriends and spend time catching up over an ice-cold Cosmo and some pasta.

If I like a restaurant, I go there all the time—and this particular establishment was the restaurant du jour. Because I am a creature of habit, I notice patterns. Every time I walked into Lunellos, I saw a tall, dark, and handsome man looking at me. He would smile, and I would walk confidently past him.

Me and Michael Enjoying A Night On The Town

This stranger would flirt. He would say hello or buy me a drink. However, I was cautious. Rumors run rampant in Jersey, and the rumor was he was a man not to mess with. He was married. This is a big NO for me. Married men are not an option. I learned this the hard way.

Once a week, at Lunellos, I found myself knee-deep in a bowl of pasta with a cocktail in my hand. The same tall, dark, and handsome gentleman would make a gesture. It would be a wink or a smile, or even a wave.

"Kim," I thought, "this guy is attractive." However, I never engaged in conversation with him.

Ritchie, the Maitre D' at Lunellos, became a dear friend of mine and would direct me to a safe space. He would offer up conversation and gossip. He became like family. Ritchie was the friendly face who welcomed me, entertained me, and suggested the best food on the menu. When his father died, I knew I had to go to the service. Mom and I were very fond of him, and we wanted to support him when he needed us the most.

We headed to the funeral service, paid our respects, and sat down in the center row. As I was reading the remembrance card, I looked up and locked eyes with that tall, dark, and handsome man from the restaurant. He was taken aback by seeing me out of our natural habitat, Lunellos. He smiled and moved on. This man, from afar, had an endearing charm. However, I reminded myself that he was off-limits. No married men for this girl!

During the days, after I worked out and before I headed over to the boutique, I found myself lounging around at my house, rifling through magazines. Between work and raising a son, reading the latest gossip was an escape. The phone rings, and it is Jimmy. You know my old boyfriend Jimmy, the one that I was addicted to.

"Kim," Jimmy begins, "Michael from the restaurant is going through a nasty divorce."

My ears perk up. "Jimmy—which guy?" I put my People Magazine on the table and began to pace. I knew it was THAT GUY, but I wanted Jimmy to tell me again.

Jimmy confirmed, "You betcha, Kim—you know the guy who is always at the bar after work." The tall, dark, handsome man is available, I thought. I couldn't concentrate on anything Jimmy was talking about. I knew the time to strike was now.

The inner dialogue in my head heightened.

*Am I ready to date?*

*Am I ready to give my heart away again?*

Tapping my fingers on the kitchen table, I became flush with excitement.

*Yes, I am ready.*

I did not want to get ahead of myself, so I made a proper plan. I was in a really good place and did not want to be anchored down with the responsibilities of a relationship. In true Kim D. fashion, I made a concerted effort to find this man, flirt like crazy, and leave it at that.

Now that I knew the tall, dark, handsome gentleman was free of marital chains, I had to find him and make it look like a coincidence. Weekly, I would get all dolled up, put on my sexiest outfits, and scan the floor at Lunellos. Every time I went to the restaurant, I would be disappointed. I could not find him anywhere.

I strutted into Lunellos and whispered into Ritchie, the Maitre D's ear, "Is he here?" He would nod no. This was proving to be a more difficult task than I thought. I began to give up on the idea of connecting with this man.

One fall evening, Mom and my stepfather, Tommy Granatell, and I were watching Christopher play football. Chris loved sports, and my parents were his biggest cheerleaders. There is something so refreshing about the bright lights in a high school stadium, wrapped up in a cozy sweater, while cheering your kid on to victory. Mom and Tommy would always make sure Chris knew they were there with their loud screams. They sat in the bleachers yelling his name and jumping up and down with each touchdown.

"Kim," Mom nudged, "Kim, you are going to be late for your dinner with the girls. Go get ready." Mom pointed at her watch and nodded. Ugh, I thought. I was tired and ready to jump into bed and watch a movie after the football game.

I was not that interested in dinner this particular evening. However, Mom's insistence was hard to ignore. I threw my arm around Mom's shoulder and gave her a peck on the cheek. "Ok, Ma, can you bring Chris home?" She nodded yes.

I believe in fate. I believe that the universe is always pointing us in a direction of where we are meant to go. We often choose to ignore these whispers, and when we do ignore these signals, our paths follow wild directions. The power of listening to the whispers of fate will nudge us towards the life we are meant to live.

I jumped in my Mercedes and raced home. "What am I going to wear?" I thought. After all, it is all about optics. We can feel tired, sad, or disengaged, yet when we look good, we attract good energy. Positive energy attracts positive energy. When we feel like crap and look like crap, we attract crap. Good attracts good, and bad attracts bad. Remember this.

I ransacked my closet, grabbed a white off-the-shoulder sweater, and dabbed red lipstick on my mouth. "Not bad for getting ready in 10 minutes," I thought.

I jumped in my car and raced over to Lunellos. I can't believe I did not get a speeding ticket that evening. I ran up to the front of the restaurant and gave Ritchie, the Maitre D, a kiss on the cheek. "Hi there! So excited for tonight!" I quipped.

Kim Granatell, my step-sister, and my attorney were waiting for me. I was not greeted with a hug or a kiss, but with wide eyes pointing to the dark, handsome man at the bar.

"OH MY GAWD," I thought to myself. "He is here." With all the bravado I could muster, I took a deep breath and walked up to him. I smiled at Kim G., confirming I understood her silent message. She knew I was going to make a "Kim D." entrance. After all, you only get one chance to make a first impression.

"Hi ya! I am so happy to see you," I gave this man I have been admiring a big kiss on the cheek. He looked at me and beamed. Later, this tall, dark, and handsome stranger told me his knees were knocking and he had to excuse himself to the bathroom. He was electrified by my bold entrance.

"So happy to see you, I was about to leave, now I have a reason to stay," He began, "I am Michael. I am so happy to see you tonight."

This was my Michael. This was the man I spent 13 magnificent years with. This was the man who supported me during the twists and turns of life. Michael was the love of my life. And it all started with a twist of fate.

Me, Michael, My Mom and Alice

"Michael," I uttered softly, with a blend of sweetness and confidence in my voice, "I'm thrilled that we've finally connected."

As the night unfolded, it felt like time slipped away, lost in the depths of each other's gaze. Amidst sips of my favorite Veuve Clicquot champagne, our conversation meandered through the vignettes of his life, his aspirations, and the serendipity that intertwined our paths on this particular evening.

I did not want to leave, yet there is a fine balance between giving too much to a guy and making him long for you even more. I knew it was time to go home. Walking me to his car, Michael drew me close. "Thank you, Michael, I am so happy we had tonight." He smiled, and he kissed me.

In that moment, I sensed something profound — a certainty that he was the man with whom I'd share my life. Another kiss sealed that unspoken pact. From my purse, I retrieved a pen and a champagne-soaked napkin. I scribbled my phone number on the napkin and gave him one last kiss.

"Call me," I whispered, and his silent nod spoke volumes. With a racing heart, I drove off into the night, hoping against hope that he felt the same irresistible pull I did.

And he did.

The next morning, at 10:30 on the dot, the phone rang and pierced the quiet of my morning. "Kim, let's do lunch," Michael's voice commanded. His pursuit was evident, and I welcomed it eagerly. I knew there was something special here. Michael and I did not play games. We knew we liked each other and that is that. Love doesn't have to be confusing or overanalyzed.

When two people really hit it off, they don't have time for games. It's all about being genuine, spending time together, and not playing around. It can be straightforward and lifegiving; this was the kind of love I was looking for. Listen to me, if someone goes silent for a whole week, it's a pretty clear sign they're not that interested. There is no need to overanalyze or wait around for them to reach out. In matters of love, actions speak louder than words. If they're not making an effort, it's best to move on and find someone who's just as enthusiastic about you as you are about them.

Michael had been living in a hotel for two years. His life was in a place of flux. He loved his family and knew his marriage was over. His hotel room was a sanctuary where he could collect his thoughts, yet he missed his children. He was a family man at his core. He would do anything for his children. And unbeknownst to me, he continued to wear his wedding ring. This did not faze me. In fact, I knew it was a symbol that he was dedicated to his children.

Our first week together was a whirlwind. We were entranced with each other. We wanted to learn everything about each other. We laughed like crazies, ate delicious food, and our make-out sessions were epic. A week after I met Michael, he wanted to take me out on a proper date. We sat cozied up in the corner of Novellis, one of our favorite Italian restaurants, and began sharing our feelings.

"Kim," Michael whispered as he grabbed my hand, "Kim, I am feeling something I have never felt before. I'm serious."

*I am listening. Michael, I am listening.*

117

"I feel like I am falling in love with you," he confessed, his eyes briefly dropping to his plate before he smiled.

"Michael," I replied, "Michael, I think I am falling for you too."

Falling in love was effortless with Michael. He was kind, smart, and funny. He was my Michael.

"Kim, I just want to be very honest with you. I am a family man. There is nothing I love more than my kids. I just need you to know that if they ask me to come back, I will do it."

I sat there for a moment, digesting what he had just revealed. "Okay, Michael," I began, "I understand. I am willing to roll the dice with you."

Mind you, we did not have sex. I am a woman who believes that there is a lot of power in what we, as women, have to offer. I am not judging, but when you give it up on the first date to a man, what more do you have to offer? There is no mystery, there is no hunger. When you jump into bed with a guy, you give up your power.

A few weeks later, Michael called me. "Kim, I am going to Atlantic City. How about it? You and me?"

He didn't have to ask me twice. I packed my bags for a weekend adventure and was ready to gamble on him. Friday afternoon, he picked me up, and we jumped into his black Audi, heading to AC. Michael grabbed my hand, and I noticed he wasn't wearing his wedding ring. Hmmmmmmm, I thought.

Atlantic City, or AC as the locals call it, is like a mashup of the Jersey Shore vibes – think boardwalks and beach days – with a sprinkle of Vegas glitz. Ever since they gave the green light to gambling back in the late '70s, it's been drawing folks who want to try their luck at the tables and maybe catch some rays in between. Plus, you've got fancy hotels, cool clubs, and swanky shops to entertain your days away.

Our trip to AC was nothing short of amazing! We pulled up to the Caesars Hotel and were escorted to a presidential suite complete with butlers, strawberries, and Veuve Clicquot.

Let me tell you why I absolutely love staying at Caesars in Atlantic City. First off, the vibe is electric. As soon as I step onto the iconic Boardwalk, I know I'm in for an unforgettable experience.

The dining options at Caesars Atlantic City are top-notch. From upscale restaurants to cozy cafes, there's always something delicious to indulge in. And when it's time to let loose, The Pool After Dark at Harrah's Resort is the ultimate party destination. The music, the atmosphere – it's pure excitement. It's a wonderland for adults.

And let's not forget about the pools. Whether I'm lounging by the transformed rooftop pool at Caesars or taking a dip in the indoor oasis at Harrah's Resort, it's pure relaxation.

Michael and I settled in. It felt very natural. We spent the day walking on the boardwalk, shopping, and sipping on coffee. We came back to our suite and settled in for a quick nap before we head out for the night. I laid my head on the pillow and gave Michael a little kiss. Michael followed up with a cryptic statement: "I'm not the man I used to be."

"Ok, Michael," I paused, "Michael, I am here for you- so let's go out and have some fun! We are in Atlantic City love!".

We decided to hit the tables for some gambling excitement. And in the midst of our adventures, we even swung by a boutique where he surprised me with a stunning white and rose wedding ring. Michael spoiled me like no other.

But the real highlight? We had an absolute blast! We were in sync. We loved the same things and adored each other.

At one point, I got a little carried away and ended up ripping my clothes off. Michael took a look at my naked body and let me tell you, we realized Michael had no problems. And would you believe it, eight days later, we made sure we were both satisfied. What started as a weekend getaway turned into a week-long extravaganza!

Michael loved to take care of me. He even loved to run a luxurious bath for me, bubbles and all. I would tear off my clothes and strut past him.

The look on his face was priceless. We created our own personal nirvana every day.

I had to pinch myself. Every night when I went to bed, I felt heady in love. Every morning when I opened my eyes, I could not believe the life I was living. I had an amazing man in my life, great friends, and a son who was thriving.

The normality of life started to sink in. The honeymoon phase was technically over, yet, we continued to have fun. I always had a bag packed because I never knew if Michael was going to plan a spontaneous trip.

Michael was full of surprises. And this guy was super supportive. He wanted the best for me. He knew me inside and out. Most importantly, he knew I loved dogs.

Michael and I enjoyed long conversations about our lives before we met to understand what made us tick. I shared with him a traumatic moment in my early days that I never recovered from. This was before Brian, Joey, Jimmy, Frank, and the rest of the big boys. This was the love affair I could not forget.

This love affair was with a puppy I never met.

I was 12 years old, and I finally convinced Mom to buy me a puppy. For years, I had been on the sidelines, dreaming of a little fur baby of my own. I was an only child for 8 years and had plenty of adult companions, yet I knew I needed a playmate of my own. I wanted to take care of my very own dog.

"Yes, Kimberlee," Mom paused and smiled, "You can have a puppy!"

"Oh mommy! THANK YOU THANK YOU!", I squealed. This was the best day of my life. I would have a best friend to greet me every day after school. I would have a sidekick, a best friend, and soulmate all wrapped up into one.

I knew exactly what dog I wanted. I wanted a Yorkshire Terrier. Again, fate intervened. Mom had a dear friend who had connections in Yorkshire, England. Mom made a few phone calls, and a puppy from Yorkshire, England would soon be placed on an airplane and headed to our home in New Jersey.

I was ready. I prepared a beautiful space in the corner of my room for my new puppy. She would have a cozy little bed next to mine so I could keep my eye on her at all times. I had spools of colorful ribbon and weaved tiny little hair clips for my new little best friend. I even scrawled out a list of names for my new puppy on a piece of paper and kept it under my pillow.

Elizabeth (as in Taylor).

Diana (as in Ross).

Sophia (as in Loren).

I would know what to name her when I held her for the first time. My puppy was escorted on a plane to Newark Airport. I counted down the days until she would be released from quarantine. Everything was perfect! Until Mom tapped on my door.

"Kimberlee, darling." Mom sat on the edge of my bed and grabbed my hand. "Darling, I am so sorry, but we cannot bring the puppy home."

I felt my face going flush. This cannot be true. "Kimberlee, my dear, your sister is allergic to dogs and we cannot bring the puppy home. Now, I want you to be a big girl and understand that sometimes we cannot have everything we want."

*LIKE HELL I CAN'T!*

Mom patted my arm, stood up, and walked out of my bedroom. I was numb. It felt like my best friend was dead and no one cared. My dreams were flushed down the toilet. I sat in my bedroom for days, crying. I hated everything about my life. All I wanted was a dog and nobody cared!

Michael cared. Michael knew my story, and he would give me dogs like most men present their girlfriends flowers. He knew animals made me happy.

One warm summer afternoon, Michael and I sat behind the 3rd base line watching our favorite baseball team, the Yankees. We were (and I still am) huge Yankees fans. Our friends were abuzz with fun conversations, and Michael's good friend mentioned to us that there was a litter of puppies on Lexington Avenue and the owner was looking for good homes. Michael grabbed my hand. "Come on, Kim, let's go get you a puppy!"

We drove over to Lexington Avenue, and I fell in love with a precious tea cup parti poodle. We named her Posche. Yes, Posche. Sixteen years later, my little Posche sits on my lap as I am writing this book.

No one will ever tell me I cannot have a dog, ever.

I grew my fur family, and Michael loved seeing me so happy. We went everywhere with our puppies. We could be spotted in the fanciest of shops and restaurants with two strollers full of my babies.

## THE END

Michael and I settled into a wonderful rhythm in our relationship, cherishing and always supporting each other. He delighted in surprising me with exciting outings, and I was always ready for the adventure.

"Kim," he said one day, "Let's get dressed up—I bought a table for the fundraiser of the year." Oh boy, this was going to be good.

"We are going to Caroline Manzo's fundraiser!"

I knew Caroline Manzo well. She was the sensible matriarch of the Manzo family, the backbone of the Brownstone, and the star of the hit reality show, Real Housewives of New Jersey. I eagerly got dolled up, anticipating an interesting evening ahead.

Michael and I strolled into the Manzos' home and were guided to their impeccably manicured backyard. A grand tent stretched across the lawn, adorned with a magical array of crystals and flowers decorating the dining tables. Cocktails flowed freely, and the food was scrumptious, with canapés filling our plates. The energy was intoxicating.

In the background, a camera crew captured all of our interactions—they were there filming an episode for Real Housewives of New Jersey. I chatted with all the ladies: Teresa, Jacqueline, Dina, and the rest of the group. Michael was particularly taken with Teresa. He admired her old-fashioned values and the fact that she was such a family-oriented person. Family meant everything to Michael, and he appreciated those same qualities in others.

Out of the corner of my eye, I saw the iconic producer Carlos King mingling with the attendees. Known affectionately as the "King of Reality TV" for his Midas touch, King had a stellar reputation. During the sixth season of The Real Housewives of Atlanta, King executive produced the highest-rated season ever, not just for the franchise but for the Bravo network as a whole.

Carlos noticed the fun I was having with the girls and made his way over to me. He pulled me aside and asked, "Kim, are you friends with Danielle Staub?"

I was curious and replied, "Well, we are acquaintances, Carlos. Why?"

He whispered, "I need a buffer. None of the girls will talk to her—you might be the perfect one for the job."

Then, with a hopeful look, he asked for my consent to film me.

Are you kidding me? Of course you have my consent!

Michael was not pleased.

The producers of RHONJ saw that "WOW" factor in me and knew I was Switzerland. I told it like it is and could balance the acidic tongues of the cast. I was all on board.

Sitting at Posche with Kristen, I felt a deep sense of camaraderie. Kristen had become my ride-or-die friend, the little sister I had always wanted. She worked for me at Posche, and as we were organizing some merchandise, when the phone rang. It was the producers with an invitation to appear on the Season 2 reunion of The Real Housewives of New Jersey in Atlantic City, a grand finale for the season.

Remembering that Michael didn't approve of my filming, I knew this would be tricky. I often snuck off to film, only for Michael to later see me on an episode and question my tactics. Despite the tension it caused, I loved interacting on reality TV.

Michael didn't think my appearances on reality TV shed a positive light on me. He was incredibly protective of both me and my reputation, always concerned about how I was portrayed. To him, the drama and sensationalism of the show didn't align with the image he had of us as a couple.

As much as I loved the thrill and interaction of reality TV, Michael's disapproval cast a shadow over my excitement. I knew he only wanted the best for me, and his protective nature was one of the things I loved about him. However, this was an opportunity I didn't want to miss. The offer from Bravo was tempting: $5,000 and a luxurious hotel stay in Atlantic City.

I tried to explain to Michael how important this was to me, but his stance was firm. He believed that my participation in the reunion would compromise my integrity and our relationship. Torn between my passion for the show and my commitment to Michael, I faced an agonizing decision. Ultimately, he gave me an ultimatum: if I chose to film, our relationship would be over.

Unsure of what to do, I turned to Kristen for advice. She had always been my confidante, and I trusted her judgment implicitly. Sitting across from her at Posche, I poured out my dilemma. Kristen listened intently, her expression thoughtful.

"Kim," she said finally, "if you don't do the show, you'll always regret it. This is a huge opportunity, and you shouldn't let fear hold you back. You love being on reality TV, and it's something you're really good at. If Michael can't support you in this, then maybe it's time to rethink things."

Her words resonated with me. Kristen was right; I didn't want to live with the regret of passing up this chance. As much as I loved Michael and valued his opinion, I knew I had to follow my own path. It was a tough decision, but deep down, I realized that staying true to myself was the most important thing.

The excitement of the reunion show was electrifying. Walking onto the set, I felt a rush of adrenaline. I couldn't wait to surprise the cast with my signature witty comments and to fully immerse myself in the drama and glamour of The Real Housewives of New Jersey. It was everything I had hoped for and more.

However, Michael was furious when he found out. His anger was palpable, and while it eventually subsided, the tension between us lingered. Despite his initial reaction, I realized I had to claim my power and autonomy. Michael and I had a lot to discuss, and although our love had always been strong, I knew it would have to withstand this friction.

Unfortunately, life had other plans. Just two months later, Michael was gone. His sudden death shattered me, leaving unresolved conversations and a profound sense of loss. As I navigated through the grief, I held on to the belief that following my passion and staying true to myself was what Michael would have ultimately wanted for me.

## JERSEY FLASHBACK

For the second reunion, I was summoned again, this time under a cloak of secrecy. They whisked me away in a car to a hotel in Long Island, keeping me sequestered from the rest of the cast. It was all hush-hush. I brought my own glam squad, and my gown, a stunning Jovani number, was a showstopper. Navy blue with a high neck adorned with crystals and an open back, the cuffs shimmered with more crystals.

As I made my grand entrance onto the stage, Andy Cohen's instructions to Teresa were clear: "Do not get off the couch." And she complied. Siggy and Dolores greeted me warmly, but the rest of the cast looked like deer caught in headlights.

The moment I took my seat, the fireworks began. Teresa and Melissa, sticking to their pact, both came at me full force. My words cut deep, pushing all the right buttons. Teresa was practically bouncing off the walls. So, I fixed her with a steely gaze and delivered a warning: "If you get off that couch one more time, you're going back where you belong!" With a flourish, I crossed my wrists adorned with crystal cuffs and declared, "Clink clink!"

## MORAL OF THE STORY

In life, it's essential to stay true to your passions and values, even when faced with opposition from those you love. Balancing personal fulfillment with the expectations of others can be challenging, but maintaining your authenticity is crucial for your happiness and growth.

Throughout my journey, I experienced moments that tested my resolve but also revealed my strength.

I vividly remember sitting with Kristen at Posche, the familiar hum of the store around us. As I wrestled with the decision to join the reunion show, Kristen's unwavering support reminded me of my own resilience. Her words gave me the courage to pursue what I loved, despite the risks involved.

Another poignant moment was when I stepped onto the set of The Real Housewives of New Jersey reunion. The bright lights and bustling energy filled me with a sense of purpose. As I delivered my witty comments, the cast's reactions confirmed that I belonged there. It was a testament to my determination to embrace my passion, even knowing the potential fallout with Michael.

Michael's anger was a storm I weathered with fortitude. Though it hurt me to see him upset, I knew that my autonomy was non-negotiable. Our discussions were tough, but each conversation was a step toward asserting my right to follow my dreams.

When Michael passed away two months later, I was devastated. Yet, in my grief, I found strength in knowing that I had honored both my love for him and my commitment to myself. His loss underscored the importance of living authentically and fully, a lesson I carry with me always.

Cherish the support of those who understand and respect your journey, and remember that true love will endure even the toughest of frictions. Ultimately, your path is yours to walk, and staying true to yourself is the greatest tribute you can pay to your own life and to those who believe in you.

# CHAPTER 10: KIM

*The One Who Is The Real Big Boy*

> *"Poor is the man whose pleasure depends*
> *on the permission of another"*
> *- Madonna*

All my life, I aspired to be a wife. I watched my mother in relationships and how they were the springboard for her release from poverty. Her third and final husband, Tommy Granatell, was the enduring kind of relationship that spanned three decades. Tommy was a supporting spouse, allowing Mom the luxuries and freedom she always desired. They supported each other in every sense of the word. Mom finally found her person.

I, on the other hand, weathered relationships that were unhealthy for me. However, each relationship provided me with a lesson.

**Dorothy - You Are Not A Victim of Your Circumstances**
**Gussy - Never Judge A Book By It's Cover**
**Butchie - Power Is Intoxicating**
**Brian - Romance Is For Real**
**Joey - We Are Right Where We Are Supposed To Be**
**Frank - You Are Worthy Of A Healthy Relationship**
**George - You Can Not Heal Others if You Don't Heal Yourself**
**Jimmy - It Is Okay To Ask For Help**

## Michael - Stay True To Yourself

### And finally, the Real Big Boy is ME.

Not until I met Michael did I know what true love meant. This is why it is so bittersweet that Michael left me after 13 years. It also taught me my greatest lesson—that I was my greatest ally.

Like the lesson from "The Wizard of Oz," Dorothy, the heroine, was always searching for something. Not until she went through hell and back and followed the yellow brick road did she realize that she always had the strength and power to live the life she dreamed of. After all, there is no place like home.

I have been to hell and back. I have seen the bowels of ferocious anger, toxicity, and manipulation. I was exposed to turmoil at an early age, and it became something that felt normal to me. After all, we as humans tend to repeat what we grow up with.

When Michael died, I realized that I am okay being alone. In fact, I thrived. I have not been in a relationship for over a decade. The pain of grief struck me like a lightning bolt, and it is a pain I wish on no one.

However, in moments of lucidity, I recognized that I did not need anyone to complete me. Can you imagine when I watched the movie "Jerry Maguire"? My eyes rolled when the actor Tom Cruise told Renée Zellweger, "You complete me." This very line caused moviegoers everywhere to believe that someone else can make you a whole person.

*Listen to me, you are the only person who can complete yourself.*

You know, growing up, we often get this idea drilled into our heads that happiness and fulfillment come from external things - like finding that one special person, reaching certain goals, or getting our hands on the latest gadgets. But here's the truth: that's a bit of a myth.

Think about it. How many times have we chased after something we thought would make us happy, only to find that it left us feeling empty or wanting more? I've been there, done that, got the T-shirt. Turns out, relying on external stuff for our happiness is like trying to fill a bucket with a hole in it - it might work for a little while, but eventually, we're left high and dry.

The real magic happens when we realize that we've got everything we need right here, inside ourselves. Yep, you heard me right - you've got the power! It's all about tuning in to what truly makes us tick, what lights a fire in our bellies, and going after it with everything we've got.

It's not always easy. Life throws curveballs, and sometimes it feels like we're swimming against the current. But here's the thing: every choice we make, every step we take, it all adds up. We're the captains of our own ships, charting our own course through the choppy waters of life.

Let's not forget about the people around us. Friends, family, partners - they're all part of the journey too. But here's the kicker: they're not there to complete us. They're there to cheer us on, to share the adventure, and to lend a hand when the going gets tough.

**WHAT THE? WHAT THE?**

Nobody can complete you. Period. You are your own BIG BOY. You have the power to live the life you want. You have the power to be your own worst enemy or your very best friend. The choice is yours.

- Be your own Dorothy and choose not to be a victim of your circumstance.
- Be your own Gussy and do not judge someone else's life until you know all the facts.
- Be your own Butchie and own your power.
- Be your own Brian, and romance the hell out of yourself.
- Be your own Joey and realize that every twist and turn in your life has led you to right where you are meant to be.
- Be your own Frank, and understand that you are worthy of goodness and you do not need to tolerate abuse.
- Be your own George, and heal yourself before you attempt to heal others.
- Be your own Jimmy, and understand that it is okay to ask for help. Asking for help is a sign of strength.
- Be your own Michael and recognize that YOUR truth is all that matters.
- And finally, be you your own Kim D., and understand that your voice matters.

Live your life with the Big Boys.
*Xo - Kim D.*

# WITH GRATITUDE

I want to thank the BIG BOYS who contributed to the completion of this book- without them, I would not have this platform to share the story that shaped my life.

Thank you to **Kerry Brett,** the photographer extraordinaire who captured my essence on the cover.

Thank you to **Angel Martin,** who captures my essence on social media and is my right hand RHONJ gossip partner on my podcast.

Thank you to my **cousin Patti** for taking trips down memory lane.

Thank you to **Tia Walden** for infusing New Jersey Flashbacks into this manuscript.

Thank you to **Yvanna Vargas,** who has been my right hand and part of my family and encourages me every step of the way.

To **Posche, Scarlett, Lyla, Bentley, Versace, Bella, Chanel and Chloe**, my little fur babies that inspire me everyday.

Thank you to **my fans, my dolls,** who have supported my truth for so many years.

# AFTERWORD

*by Margaret Josephs*

Housewives is the least
interesting thing about Kim D
and that says alot f

XO
MARGARET
JOSEPHS
Margaret Josephs

Soirée
your way

#  AFTERWORD

*by John Fuda*

There are few individuals who possess the unique blend of qualities that define Kim D. What truly sets Kim apart is her ability to not just compete but dominate in arenas typically reserved for the most formidable big boy players. In every aspect of her life, Kim approaches challenges with a directness and clarity that are both refreshing and effective. She cuts through the noise with precision, always focused on the task at hand and unafraid to confront the toughest obstacles head-on. From the outset, Kim's story is one of resilience and authenticity. Her grounded nature and unassuming demeanor belie a strength and tenacity that have propelled her to the forefront of her industry, inspiring others to follow in her footsteps and redefine success on their own terms. Kim's unwavering commitment to her values and relentless pursuit of excellence serve as a beacon of inspiration for aspiring entrepreneurs everywhere. But perhaps most impressive is Kim's toughness—a quality that has earned her respect and admiration in even the most male-dominated spaces. She doesn't just survive in these environments; she thrives, proving time and again that she is more than capable of holding her own against the biggest players in the game. And through it all, Kim remains humble—a rare trait in someone of her stature. She never seeks the spotlight or the accolades, preferring instead to let her work speak for itself. It is this humility, coupled with her unwavering dedication, that truly sets her apart. As you read through the pages of this book, I encourage you to reflect on the lessons and insights that Kim has to offer. Her story is not just one of success, but of perseverance, resilience, and the unwavering belief that anything is possible with hard work and determination.

# 💋 ABOUT KIM DE PAOLA

Kim De Paola, a New Jersey icon brings style, compassion, and authenticity which has built the foundation for a remarkable career spanning over three decades.

Kim De Paola, affectionately known as Kim D., is a multifaceted personality recognized for her appearances on *The Real Housewives of New Jersey (RHONJ)*. However, her influence extends far beyond the realm of reality television. Kim is a devoted animal advocate, a loving mother, a fashion icon, and the host of the popular podcast, *Get Real With Kim D.*

At the heart of Kim's endeavors is her unwavering love for animals. A passionate advocate for animal rights, she tirelessly supports rescue organizations and raises awareness about pet adoption and welfare through her platform. Kim's commitment to making a difference in the lives of animals is a testament to her compassionate nature and unwavering dedication to causes close to her heart.

As a mother, Kim De Paola exudes warmth and strength, serving as a guiding force for her family. Her close bond with her son reflects her nurturing spirit and fierce maternal instincts, demonstrating the depth of her love and support.

In the world of fashion, Kim De Paola stands as a beacon of style and sophistication. As the owner of Posche Boutique, she curates an exquisite collection of high-end fashion pieces that showcase her impeccable taste and keen eye for trends. Kim's influence as a fashion icon inspires others to embrace their unique sense of style and confidence.

Adding to her repertoire, Kim hosts the podcast *Get Real With Kim D*, where she invites listeners to join her in candid conversations about life, love, and everything in between. Through her podcast, Kim shares her wisdom, experiences, and unfiltered perspective, offering listeners a glimpse into her world and leaving a lasting impression.

Join Kim De Paola on a journey of empowerment, compassion, and style. Whether she's advocating for animals, nurturing her family, or sharing her insights on her podcast, Kim's authenticity and passion shine through, leaving an indelible mark on all who encounter her.

Thank you for stepping into the world of Kim De Paola, where every moment is an opportunity to live authentically, love fiercely, and make a difference.

Follow Kim on Instagram: @kimdposche
Check out Kim's Website: www.poschebykimd.com

# ABOUT JULIE LOKUN

Julie Lokun, JD, is an international best-selling author celebrated for her influential works such as "Audiocasters," "Hustle Smart," and "Cre8tive Con." Her literary contributions have resonated with readers worldwide, establishing her as a formidable voice in the realm of personal development and creative entrepreneurship.

In addition to her writing, Julie is a top podcaster, known for her highly acclaimed podcast "Obsessed With Humans on the Verge of Change." This podcast ranks in the top 1% globally, a testament to its impact and the compelling content that captivates a diverse audience.

Julie is also the dynamic founder of The Mediacasters, a media firm dedicated to amplifying voices and transforming the way stories are told. Her leadership in this venture underscores her commitment to innovation and excellence in media.

Balancing her professional achievements, Julie is a devoted wife and mother of four boys, whose lively household also includes two cherished French Bulldogs. Her ability to juggle her bustling career with her vibrant family life showcases her extraordinary dedication and multifaceted talents.

Follow Julie on Instagram: @julie_lokun

Check out Julie's website: www.julielokunconsulting.com

Cher, Michael and Me

Mom, Me and Andy Cohen

Paul Anka and Me

Made in the USA
Middletown, DE
12 June 2024

55524734R10099